# To Walk in Heaven's Light

## Dr. C.R. Hill, Jr.

To Walk in Heaven's Light
Published by Yawn's Publishing
2555 Marietta Hwy, Ste 103
Canton, GA 30114
www.yawnspublishing.com

Library of Congress Control Number: 2017914578

ISBN: 978-1-947773-03-5   paperback
       978-1-947773-04-2   eBook

Printed in the United States

# Foreword

Jean Cocteau wrote, "The poet doesn't invent. He listens." For over 50 years, Reverend C. R. Hill has listened - listened to his parishioners, listened to his friends, listened to his family. He has woven his life into theirs as trusted pastor, spiritual guide, and Christian leader. For many of his parishioners, he was given the privilege of speaking at their funeral. In those moments when life's evening shadows fell, C. R.'s eulogies became poetry.

The poems in *To Walk in Heaven's Light* are accounts of lives well lived. They are stories of love, stories of struggle, stories of some who lived long faithful years and others whose lives were halted far too soon. You will read tributes to mothers and fathers, children, those in the military, musicians, teachers, athletes and more; some who experienced great success, and some who left this world feeling the weight of failure.

For family and friends left to mourn, Rev. Hill's poem is balm to soothe their soul. Many have said good-bye after months and years of caring for one who suffered with an illness that would not let go. They are weary. Others received phone calls, or the alarming knock at the door, in the middle of the night informing them of a tragic death. They are shocked. Like a pastor who sits by the bedside, C. R.'s poems comfort.

"To Walk in Heaven's Light" stirs our emotions as we glimpse into lives we never knew. The poems not only comfort, they chronicle. The words remind us of the details of their lives, the point in history when they lived, and sweet traits that won't soon be forgotten. More importantly though, Reverend Hill offers hope. Each poem ending with the truth that we can all soon walk in Heaven's light through the grace of God in Jesus Christ.

I've now caught the view from the top of the hill,
Heaven's beauty before me I now see,
The glory exceeds all on earth I had dreamed,
And best of all, here comes Jesus for me.

Dr. Kina S. Mallard
President of Reinhardt University

# Dedicated to Jackie Hill
## My Faithful Wife of Over Fifty-Four years

Jacqueline Ward Daniel Hill – Jackie and I met on a blind date on a Friday or Saturday night in June 1962. Her cousin had arranged it, and Jackie said she would go out with me once, but no more than one date. Our second date was that same weekend, she went to church with me that Sunday evening, and we dated steadily for five months then we married. I knew the moment I first saw her that she would be the woman I would marry.

Many of our dates were going to church or church activities. I had experienced a dramatic encounter with Jesus in April 1962 after having fought bitterly against the call of God on my life for eight years. My proposal to her came on a date we both though would be our last – we each left our homes that night thinking we would break up with the other. I think we must have gone to church and afterwards we were talking about God and the church when I said to her, "I know that God has something for me to do and when I find out what it is I am going to have to go and do it. Do you want to come along?" That was my proposal. She did not say yes or no, she just kissed me and I took that for a yes.

That call of God became clear on the following Palm Sunday morning when I had delivered the morning message as a Lay Speaker at the Bostwick Methodist Church in Bostwick Ga. I told her as we drove out of the parking lot after that service that I knew then what I had to do.

I was a high school dropout with a GED that I got while in the army. I told our pastor that God was calling me to be a preacher, started to Athens Business School is September, and started assisting the pastor of the Crawford Circuit in two of his four churches that same fall. In June of 1964, I started in Summer School at The University of Georgia, and I received my first appointment to two churches on the Athens Circuit in the Athens Elberton District of what was then still The Methodist Church., later to become The United Methodist Church. Through eleven years of going to school and pastoring churches, another thirty-seven of full-time pastoral ministry, and five years of part-time hospital chaplaincy, Jackie was there. She was faithfully at my side supporting, supplementing, and sustaining me and my ministry as she quietly went about influencing and changing the lives of others through her own unique ministry in Jesus Christ her Lord.

I retired from pastoral ministry in June of 2011. We learned that Jackie had cancer in July. She fought that for five and a half years before it killed her body. It never conquered her spirit. Jackie had no illusions about life on this earth. She loved life and she loved people. She loved Jesus and she loved the church. She loved teaching Women's Bible Studies and the ladies in her classes. She loved music, and could sing just about every song in the hymnal without looking at the book. For all of that she knew that life on this earth was temporary. She never complained about having cancer. Most of the people who knew her did not know she had cancer, or if they did they had no idea how bad it really was. She maintained that it was what it was and she would deal with it. If anyone asked how she was, her answer was always "I am fine." She was fine because as she said to me, when we were on our way to the hospital for a scan a few days before she died, "C. R. I am fine and you are fine. We will get through this, and if not I will be with Jesus and I will be fine and you will be fine." "I Am Fine" Those words are engraved in stone on her marker, and she is fine because she is with Jesus in that house, not made with hands, eternally in the heavens.

# She Walks in Heaven's Light

Through the years she faithfully walked,
Holding Jesus' hand and mine;
Until we reached the water's edge,
Where she stepped beyond the shores of time.

Oh the love she drew from God,
Then passed along to me,
As together we served his flocks,
On this side of heaven's sea.

Her beauty I did daily view,
Radiant with God's grace;
While in her quiet steady ways,
I discerned the image of God's face.

The faith we shared these many years,
Has been our anchor through life's storms.
And though in faith I give her up.
I yet long to hold her in my arms.

I yearn once more to see her face,
And to have her by my side;
So I will keep this path we've trod,
Until I too, step over Jordan's tide.

While in the wake of the life she lived,
I will yet other souls invite,
To place their hand in Jesus' palm,
Then walk by faith in heaven's light.

C. R. Hill, Jr.
Copyright 12/27/16

In Loving memory of
Jacqueline (Jackie) W. Hill
My wonderful wife of 54 years

# Introduction

TO WALK IN HEAVEN'S LIGHT is a collection of two hundred and fifty-four memorial poems that I have written for the funeral and memorial services of church members, their families, and friends over more than three decades. These poems are the ones that I still have in my records. Sadly, there are a number of poems that I have written during these years that I no longer have copies of in my files. It is to those persons whose poems have been lost from my records that the final poem, "To the Master of the March" is dedicated.

The costume of writing a poem in memory of each person whose funeral or memorial service I conducted began while I was Minister of Missions and Evangelism at Conyers First United Methodist Church in Conyers, Georgia. We had in that congregation a member named Marelon Wander, a dear sweet very quiet lady who never failed to be in church every time the doors opened for worship. She seldom ever spoke unless spoken to; she never served on any committees, or to my knowledge, did any of the things normally associated with great churchmanship. But she was always there for worship.

When Marelon died I was asked by her family to conduct her funeral service. As I was preparing the message I thought it might be nice to write a poem for her service. I had been writing poems for other occasions for some time. So, I wrote a poem celebrating her life and read it as a part of the message for her funeral. The problem with that decision was that one does not write a poem for the funeral of one church member and not write one for the funeral of the next church member, their family member, or their friend. Thus, it is a quiet little lady named Marelon Wander who was used by the Holy Spirit that is responsible for the 254 poems in this collection and the many others not available for this publication. Of course, ultimately all of the credit must go to God who through the Holy Spirit is the true source of each poem. When Jesus was making his triumphant entry into Jerusalem as his followers sang his praises, the Pharisees asked him to make the crowds stop praising him. Jesus replied, "I tell you that, if these should hold their peace, the stones would immediately cry out." Luke 19: 40 KJV. Therefore, if any good, any comfort, any hope or inspiration comes from these poems then give God the credit for I am only a stone with a pen.

In closing let me say a word about the cover. The pictures of the sunsets were taken at Lake Junaluska, the United Methodist Assembly Grounds in Maggie Valley North Carolina. Lake Junaluska was one of my wife's favorite places on this earth to spend time. The picture of the lady walking in the clouds towards the light is my wife. That picture of her walking was taken while we were vacationing on Mackinac Island the year before she was diagnosed with cancer. She was walking up toward the Grand Hotel, a place she had always dreamed of experiencing. So, you see the symbolism is my beloved wife walking from the place on earth she loved to the mansion in heaves that she knew through her faith that Jesus had prepared for her.

C. R. Hill, Jr.

# To Those Remembered

| Name | Poem | Page |
|------|------|------|
| Alexander, John Lafayette | The Ripples In God's Palm | 1 |
| Amos, Lydia Jo | Heaven's Diamonds | 2 |
| Anderson, James R | The Resting of a Soldier | 3 |
| Anderson, Martha Marie | A Queen In Servant's Attire | 4 |
| Anderson, Wendell | He Will Forever Each One Know | 5 |
| Arnold, Sara Barber | Beyond The Whispered Years | 6 |
| Arnold, William C. | The Call of the Distant Lights | 7 |
| Attaway, Johnny | God's Stage Where Life Goes On | 8 |
| Austin, Allene | At the Master Servant's Feet | 9 |
| Austin, John Byron | Where Life is Young Again | 10 |
| Bacon John | Each One He Made His Own | 11 |
| Bagwell Randall | Well Done | 12 |
| Bagwell, Wayne Sr | The Garden Gate | 13 |
| Ballenger, Bill | An Ode to Valor | 14 |
| Bankston Benny & Frances | Beyond the Fields of Brown | 15 |
| Bankston, Joel B | The Runner | 16 |
| Bannister, Jewell Wyatt | The Priceless Jewel | 17 |
| Barger, William and Mitch | Flying | 18 |
| Beck, Paul | Around the Upward Bend | 19 |
| Berwald Annabelle | Life at Road's End | 20 |
| Biddle Carol | The Anchors of God's Grace | 21 |
| Blumenaus, John | The Homeland of the Soul | 22 |
| Boling, Fred | The Music of His Life | 23 |

| Name | Poem | Page |
|------|------|------|
| Bowden, Aubrey Marie | The Angel to Us Loaned | 24 |
| Brandenburg, Mabel M | A Saint Has Transferred Home | 25 |
| Breeding, Earnie | The Harbor of God's Arms | 26 |
| Bridges, Martha Franklin | The Crossing | 27 |
| Briscoe, Ruth Evans | In God's Eternal Book | 28 |
| Brisendine, John William | From the Top of the Hill | 29 |
| Britt, Terri | It Is Finished | 30 |
| Brodnax, Sarah Leora | On the Death of a Teacher | 31 |
| Brown, James Maxwell Jr | A Giant I Recall | 32 |
| Bryant, Pam | Her Songs Will Keep On Ringing | 33 |
| Buffington, Herbert Luther Jr. | The Quiet Man and Heaven's Son | 34 |
| Burch, Marge | Across the Finish Line | 35 |
| Butler, Mimi Jo | The Teacher and the Saint | 36 |
| Caldwell, Andrew Leonard | From the Topside Down | 37 |
| Caldwell, Ellene Louise | From Papa's Cotton Basket | 38 |
| Cannon, David Lee | Beholding God's Eternal Dawn | 39 |
| Cannon, Emma Sue Tippens | With Heaven's Path Conformed | 40 |
| Cannon, Sharon | To a 'Homegoing' Queen | 41 |
| Cantrell, Etta White | At Home Where the Angle Sings | 42 |
| Cantrell, Roger Lynn | As the Eagle's Strength Renew | 43 |
| Carlton, Christopher Edward | Beyond the Forest Dark | 44 |
| Carroll, Odell Edwin | Gone To Be With God | 45 |
| Carter, Edward P | Like the Master Archer's Arrow | 46 |

| Name | Poem | Page |
|---|---|---|
| Carter, Jane | Lady Jane | 47 |
| Cates, Laura Hamilton | In Heaven's Mansion Grand | 48 |
| Cates, Paul Sr. | The Keel That Keeps Us True | 49 |
| Cathy, Louise R. | By Nature's Ancient Bridge | 50 |
| Chambers, Anna Elizabeth | She Danced into Heaven with a Smile | 51 |
| Chambers, Mary Knight | The Summit Reached | 52 |
| Chandler, Lou Anne | Evening's Homeward Call | 53 |
| Clark, Diana Kay | In the Memory of Her Love | 54 |
| Clark, J. Norman | The Graduate | 55 |
| Clark, Virginia Ray V. A. | In the House His Love Designed | 56 |
| Claxton, Frances Rowan | A Lady Following Jesus | 57 |
| Clifford, Melinda Lewis | Fast in the Master's Hand | 58 |
| Clifford, Sandra Gail | When the Heart Will Sing and Dance | 59 |
| Coan, Charles W. | Salute to a Quiet Man | 60 |
| Cook, Hugh Burch | Birch Cook's Store | 61 |
| Corbett, Anne Elizabeth | Off Again | 62 |
| Cowan, Geneva Emma | When Came Her Crossing Time | 63 |
| Cox, Jerry | In the Light that Christmas Brings | 64 |
| Crow, Donald | Evening Time at Home | 65 |
| Crumpler, George A. | On the Wings of Fluid Grace | 66 |
| Dalais, Rosa Emma | In You Her Song Lives On | 67 |
| Daniel, Samuel Jack | With Jesus I've Gone Fishing | 68 |
| Davis, Jami E | If for a Moment One Believes | 69 |
| DeMore, Coyle A | The Gates of Heaven Gained | 70 |

| Name | Poem | Page |
|------|------|------|
| DeMore, Eleanor | Heaven's Gain | 71 |
| Dettner, Marry Alice | In Strength She Now Is Dancing | 72 |
| DeVan Jim | An Amplifying Echo | 73 |
| DeVan, Jim | A Man from Heaven Sent | 74 |
| Duncan, Major W. L. | At Heaven's Morning Roll Call | 75 |
| Edge, Anne | Heaven Bound On the Evening Breeze | 76 |
| Edge, Carl | When you Meet in Heaven's Dawn | 77 |
| Elliott, Frankie | Heaven's Porch Light | 78 |
| Ellis, Marie | Taking Leave in Autumn | 79 |
| Farrell, Harry G. | The Music of His Life | 80 |
| Ferrell, Charles Maurice | In My Eternal Strength | 81 |
| Fife, Sue Weaver | In the House of God's Abode | 82 |
| Fincher, Frances | A Mountain Flower Blooming | 83 |
| Fincher, Jack Chamber Jr | A Fisherman's Farewell | 84 |
| Fincher, Katherine | Through Ageless Seasons Singing | 85 |
| Floyd, Mabel Trellis | With the Christmas Christ Now Gone | 86 |
| Ford, James Richard | On The Wings of Grace | 87 |
| Foster, Emerson Parks | In Heaven's Finished Room | 88 |
| Fuetus, Betty | A House Not Made With Hands | 89 |
| Gardner, Jane Elliott | I'll Meet You At The River | 90 |
| Gibson, Horace Eugene Jr. | Heaven's Glad Tomorrow | 91 |
| Gibson, Mary Agnes | With Happy Memories Dear | 92 |
| Glass, Allen Howard | On Morning's Wings | 93 |
| Gleaton, William Horace | Papa's House | 94 |

| Name | Poem | Page |
|------|------|------|
| Goodman, Bessie Mays | A Light Still Shining | 95 |
| Gorham, Margret Louise | Margaret's Song | 96 |
| Gray, Charlotte | Diamonds on the Cheek | 97 |
| Gray, Veachel Loyd | To God's Eternal Day | 98 |
| Gunter, Jim | From All His Labors Rested | 99 |
| Halpin, Frank Sr | Fishing With God's Son | 100 |
| Hamilton, Fannie | To Heaven's Shore | 101 |
| Hamilton, George | Someday Will Be Homecoming | 102 |
| Hammarstrom, Flow M. | In Gardens of Glory | 103 |
| Hammond, Graydon | A Champion Now At Home | 104 |
| Haney, J. B. Jr. | The Fording of Heaven's Stream | 105 |
| Haney, Meena | In Tribute to a Steel Magnolia | 106 |
| Hannah, Seth | A Runner's Early Finish | 107 |
| Harbin, Winfred | In God's Never Ending Day | 108 |
| Hardeman, Elizabeth | On the Wings of Evening's Wind | 109 |
| Harris, Virginia McAdams | Sailing From the Shores of Time | 110 |
| Harris, William Glaze | Christmas Day in the Evening | 111 |
| Harrison, Robert Michael | The Anchors of God's Grace | 112 |
| Hasty, Hazel Bonnie | With Eagle's Wings She Flies | 113 |
| Hattendorf, Wilbur S | Rejoicing on the Dance Floor | 114 |
| Hawkins, James Robert Sr. | The Sailing of a Saint | 115 |
| Hayes, Courtney | Today in Heaven I Wear a Smile | 116 |
| Haygood, Ellis | God's Home of Endless Day | 117 |

| Name | Poem | Page |
|------|------|------|
| Hightower, Clinton Sr. | His Love Runs With You Still | 118 |
| Hill, Carl Richard Sr. | Among the Hills of Time | 119 |
| Hill, Daniel Henry | The Resetting of the Sails | 120 |
| Hill, Jacqueline (Jackie) W. | She Walks in Heaven's Light | 121 |
| Hill, Louise V. | At the Water's Edge | 122 |
| Hime, Virginia Nelson | Sailing with the Evening Tide | 123 |
| Hinman, Christine | A Saint with No Fear | 124 |
| Hogan, Jack | He Played the Game for God | 125 |
| Hull, Byrd | The Home with Heaven's View | 126 |
| Hutchings, Gretta | On the Passing of a Friend | 127 |
| Jago, Norman | The Homeward Leading Lane | 128 |
| Jago, Vivian | The Lady Has Gone Home | 129 |
| Jinks, Sarah E. | Tomorrow's Heavenly Morning Dew | 130 |
| Joiner, Julia May | Her Mansion on Heaven's Side | 131 |
| Jones, George | The Homecoming | 132 |
| Jones, Vera May Haley | Come Home Now Child | 133 |
| Jones, Jane Colleen Schalf | In the Echo of Heart's Love | 134 |
| Joyner, Charles Johnny | The Well Blessed Man | 135 |
| Kelly, Howard Rae | An Airman's Final Flight | 136 |
| Kimball, Vivian Elizabeth | Living on Life's Second Page | 137 |
| King, Arnold Nathan | This Hero | 138 |
| Krueger, August | God's Tomorrow | 139 |
| Lanford, Robert A. | Fishing With Big Bob | 140 |
| Langston, James Donald | A Familiar Home and Crown | 141 |

| Name | Poem | Page |
|------|------|------|
| Langston, Mary Jane | In God's Homecoming Court. | 142 |
| Lathem, Dot | On A Bright November Day | 143 |
| Lewis, Hugh Neal | A Man Like His Mountains of Home | 144 |
| Linch, Kathryn | The Impressions of a Saint | 145 |
| London, Melvin Dale | The Biggest Race of All | 146 |
| Lovell, Forrest W. | Where Saints Immortal Stand | 147 |
| Lovell, Nell Cook | As the Saints in Order Go | 148 |
| Martin, James L. (Jim) | The Echo of His Soul | 149 |
| Martin, J. Lamar | A Dream for Children's Sake | 150 |
| McClure Earl | The Sendoff of A Friend | 151 |
| McCurry Harris | Salute to a Christian Gentleman | 152 |
| McCurry Shirley Ann | In God's Distant Promise Land | 153 |
| McDaniel, Bobby | From the Trackless Wood Emerged | 154 |
| McDaniel, Joyce Elizabeth | Joyce's Song | 155 |
| McGarity, Harold L. | Come Home 'Preacher' | 156 |
| McVay, Birch G | Marching Orders Received | 157 |
| McVay, Hilda L. | Whispers of Reveille | 158 |
| McVay, Mary Elizabeth | Until Reunion Day | 159 |
| Mercer, Elizabeth "Judy" | The Homecoming | 160 |
| Metcalf, Jordin Merit | On the Crossing of Jordin | 161 |
| Milford, Norma Ann | I'll See You Again | 162 |
| Milford, Turk John | The Shadow of a Giant | 163 |
| Miller, Anita Rooks | In the Father's Loving Palm | 164 |
| Miller, Carl | Going By His Place | 165 |

| Name | Poem | Page |
|---|---|---|
| Milton, Sallie | Precious in God's Sight | 166 |
| Moore, Betty | From Water's Edge to Heaven's Shore | 167 |
| Moore, Marion Helm | Passing Through | 168 |
| Moore, Paul Wesley | The Master of Mended Souls | 169 |
| Morgan, James H. "Jay" | On Heaven's Golden Street | 170 |
| Morris, Danny | In the Life Beyond Tomorrow | 171 |
| Moses, Quentin | Always Looking Up | 172 |
| Myatt, Edna R. | Finally Home | 173 |
| Naffziger, Beth | In the Resurrection Morning | 174 |
| Nale, Frank Winton | A Father's Steps | 175 |
| Nichols, William | Born to Rise Eternal | 176 |
| Owen, John Walker | The Voice of the Morning Breeze | 177 |
| Parham, Ellen Irene | By the Christmas Baby's Voice | 178 |
| Peacock, Dorothy | The Home Jesus Built Above | 179 |
| Peacock, Harry | With the Master Pilot | 180 |
| Peek, Dot | The Passing of a Lady | 181 |
| Peek, Roy | Friends with a Saint | 182 |
| Peterson, Sylvia | Heaven's Summer Garden Room | 183 |
| Phillips, Aaron Paul | Measure Twice, Saw Once | 184 |
| Pickett, Donald Lamar | Grieve Not My Love | 185 |
| Polk, C. O. Jack | A Name That Stood For More | 186 |
| Powell, Gladys | Around the Last Corner | 187 |
| Price, J. P. | The Model Man | 188 |
| Rainer, Robert Andrew | Taken Flight with the Autumn Leaves | 189 |
| Ray, Dorothy | On the Wings of God | 190 |

| Name | Poem | Page |
|------|------|------|
| Ray, Joseph Pierce, Jr. | Sitting Delighted at God's Table | 191 |
| Ray, Marjorie Pague | A Chat On Heaven's Porch | 192 |
| Reed, Sherry | Her Gold Refined | 193 |
| Reider, Josh | The Crown Through Jesus Won | 194 |
| Reisert, Rick Alan | His View from Above the Clouds | 195 |
| Reynolds, Roy Henry | On Silent Wings He Flew | 196 |
| Rhodes, Becky | Home by the Higher Way | 197 |
| Richards, Ellis Hampton | The Christ-Learned Way | 198 |
| Richards, Tracey Gail | Anchors for the Soul | 199 |
| Roberts, Virginia Lee | Beyond Autumn's Clear Blue Sky | 200 |
| Rooks, James | One By One on Heaven's Shore | 201 |
| Rooks, Mary Grace | A Steep from Time to Heave Go | 202 |
| Rowland, Barbara | In the Hymns of Hope and Heaven | 203 |
| Sawyer, Eugenia Hodges | In Heaven with Her Pilot | 204 |
| Scott, Brenelle Mobley | In Heaven's Pastures Green | 205 |
| Sellars, Mike | Crossing the Silver Tide | 206 |
| Shackelford, Mildred Smith | The Reunion | 207 |
| Shackelford, Stinson | Beyond the Far Horizon | 208 |
| Shankles, Jean | From Better Jesus Knowing. | 209 |
| Shankles, Loyd Bascom | Going on in the Greatness of Grace | 210 |
| Shankles, Velma | A Ransomed Spirit's Prayer | 211 |
| Shaw, Edgar | The Heavenly Voyager | 212 |
| Smith, Mary Jean | In Celebration of Life | 213 |
| Smith Ray | A Kinsman of the King | 214 |

| Name | Poem | Page |
|---|---|---|
| Smith, Richard Jackson | His Spirit Sought the Sky | 215 |
| Smith, David | God's Eternal Living Game | 216 |
| Smith, Glenda Echols | The Doorway to God's Best | 217 |
| Smith, Kathryn | At Heaven's Open Door | 218 |
| Sparks, John Sr. | In Heaven's Arms | 219 |
| Stackhouse, H. Collin | The Captain's Voyage | 220 |
| Stackhouse, Jennie T. | Before The Crystal Sea | 221 |
| Stitt, Jimmy | Forever at Christmas Home | 222 |
| Stone, Helen | The Artist's Hands | 223 |
| Strawn, Grace | Moved Home | 224 |
| Strawn, William Laurie | The Candy Man's Gone Home | 225 |
| Strickland, William Andrew (Drew) | He Lives | 226 |
| Stubbs, Robert S. II | Semper Fi, Always Faithful | 227 |
| Tarrh, Francis Michael | On Heaven's Path Sublime | 228 |
| Terrill, Ray | Now Does Soar His Soul | 229 |
| Turner, James Roy (Jimmy) | Send Back the Angel's Song | 230 |
| Underwood, Daniel Patrick | In Tribute to a Peacemaker | 231 |
| Velandia, Anais Marie | A Promise Whispered Soft | 232 |
| Wallace, Hubert (Doss) | Treasure in Heaven | 233 |
| Walter, David | Gods Eternal Day | 234 |
| *Wander, Marelon* | Sailing Glad and Graceful | 235 |
| Ward, Thaddeus Anthony | Until the Children All Get Home | 236 |
| Ward, Lemma | From the House on Hampton Street | 237 |
| Warren, Steve | Today in Heaven Found | 238 |

| Name | Poem | Page |
|------|------|------|
| Welch, Hunter | Until You Reach Heaven's Home | 239 |
| Wesley, Rick | Come Home with Me Today | 240 |
| White, Milton Thomas | The Voyager's Rest | 241 |
| Willis, Charles G. | The Captain of Souls | 242 |
| Wilson, Gladys | The Little While | 243 |
| Woods, Harry | In Unbroken Step | 244 |
| Wynn, Lee F. Sr. | Yonder Heaven's Gate | 245 |
| Yarbrough Doris | The Echo on the Breeze | 246 |
| Yarbrough, Kathy | Crossing Time | 247 |
| Yawn, Aubrey Dewitt | The Wrencher | 248 |
| Yeckering, Josh | O Heed the Somber Notes | 249 |
| Yohe, Iris Hope | One Desire Alone She Held | 250 |
| Young, Charlotte | Walking with Jesus at Dawn | 251 |
| Young, Michael Neil | The Father's Homeward Call | 252 |
| Zachary, Jean M. | Jean | 253 |
| To Those Whose Poems Were Not Available for this Collection | To the Master of the March | 254 |

## The Ripples in God's Palm

Was ever there a man of faith,
Any more assured than he,
That atop the final hill of time,
He'd view God's eternity?

O what view from Pisgah's heights,
Could in him instill such calm?
Did he discern the hills of time,
As but the ripples in God's palm?

Of course, it was on such a view,
He did through his life rely.
For he had found in Jesus Christ,
God's grace his full supply.

Did not we find in his bold trust,
As will our faith increase?
Did not we in our bedside watch,
From him acquire a kind of peace?

Yea, when the final crest of time,
Is ours to scale in trust,
May in the ripples of God's palm,
Like his our hands be thrust.

Dr. C.R. Hill, Jr.

## Heaven's Diamonds

The rock upon I've always leaned,
The one who always made things right,
Suddenly now has been removed,
And to heaven has taken flight.

Oh the weight her going leaves,
The pain is much too much to bear,
Always in my darkest night,
My rock, my mom was always there.

Now when darkness seems so strong,
When no moon or stars give light,
I wonder who will take my hand,
To lead me back to morning bright.

Then in my midnight's stillness deep,
A voice within me starts to speak.
"I am the Rock on which she leaned,
And you my child I'll always keep."

"So as the rock she was for you,
I am shaping you my child to be.
That in the nights that others face,
They might in you a beacon see."

"Rocks my child are never made,
In sunny fields by gentle rain.
But from the fires of deep distress,
Come the diamonds that heaven gain."

## The Resting of a Soldier

A soldier long returned from war,
Yet always in the fight,
Would stand up for Lord and land,
With all his earthly might.

The battle scars he bore within,
Were not from bomb or gun,
But from the long and arduous race,
That he through his life had run.

A generous man of great degree,
In that sacred order's clan.
He would let no detail go undone,
In any work done by his hand.

He walked along this path of life,
With Jesus at his side.
Though not perfect yet he knew,
That it was for him that Jesus died.

So now has come the end of day,
When life's evening shadows fall,
And those go home to live with God,
Who did in their day on Jesus call.

Dr. C.R. Hill, Jr.

## A Queen In Servant's Attire

O let this mind be found in you,
That was also in our Lord,
Who being found in human form,
Did with the servants find accord.

Then faithful even unto death,
When on a cross he died in shame,
God did place him on his throne,
With creation's highest name.

'Twas this directive from God's word,
That did this dear servant inspire,
For she truly was throughout her life,
A queen in servant's attire.

Her humble way of attentive care,
As on others she did wait,
Will now return to grace her crown,
When she enters heaven's gate.

Then kneeling at the throne of God,
That crown she'll gladly place,
Down at the feet of Jesus Christ,
Who saved her by his grace.

Then she will rise with heaven's host,
To join that joyful hymn,
And walk the golden streets of love,
Where she'll ne'er taste death again.

# He Will Forever Each One Know

He thought he was a has-been,
But that would never do,
He was and is and always will,
Be a man whose life was true.

As a man who stood for justice,
A spokesman for the weak,
He was a friend you trusted,
Whenever he did speak.

He walked among the mighty,
Yet with a humble caring stride,
Always with the knowledge,
Of Jesus walking at his side.

In faithfulness he worshiped,
And served within God's house,
And lived with equal faithfulness,
For his children and his spouse.

And when it came to dying,
Leaving loved ones here behind,
No fears or regrets beset him,
For to heaven he was resigned.

He knew that in God's morning,
All his loves of earth below,
He would see again with Jesus,
And would forever each one know.

# Beyond The Whispered Years

Swift the years have whispered by,
Since our 'Bo' was just a girl,
Now she's stepped across the bar,
As heaven's scenes unfurl.

'Twas on a cool October morning,
When Charlie crossed ahead,
Almost sixty years had whispered by,
Since the day he and 'Bo' were wed.

'Bo' tarried here four years and some,
Her life's journey to complete,
Now reunited beyond whispered years,
They stroll heaven's golden street.

On Jonesboro Street the familiar house,
Almost speaks and seems to say,
"The lives that 'Bo' and Charlie built here,
Whispered years can't steal away."

For here 'Bo' and Charlie much in love,
Took Jesus to be their guide,
They built their lives on faith in Christ,
Now they with Jesus do reside.

## The Call of the Distant Lights

Charlie Arnold put out today,
On that immortal crystal sea.
He lived on earth an example true,
To the best men were made to be.

No fear or grief delayed his voyage,
'Twas but love that held him near,
Until the lights of that distant shore,
Outshone the lights o'er here.

Ah, we awake to a chilly morn,
With some clouds obscuring the sun,
But he awoke to heaven's warmth,
Where his race was finished and won.

Look back upon the way he came,
And the path along which he trod.
Then know the key to his victorious voyage,
Was that he walked with God.

You and I should like him be,
With our lives which until we're through,
Become the people God had in mind,
When He died for me and you.

## God's Stage Where Life Goes On

A new millennium began today,
As time turned another page,
And having seen the old one out,
Johnny turned and left the stage.

Long for him life's drama ran,
And to us he was a star,
For the light of Jesus shone in him,
Touching people near and far.

A gracious man of modest means,
Not of the pulpit pounding breed,
He would go about in gentle ways,
Sharing Jesus through a deed.

He played his role with faithfulness,
He never missed a curtain call,
In the gathered cast at the house of God,
He could be found among them all.

Johnny took life's final bow,
As a new century began to dawn,
He'd finished his dress rehearsal,
For God's stage where life goes on.

## At The Master Servant's Feet

A servants heart she had within,
It was for others she did live,
Her days of toil received no pay,
But for the joy she did give.

Many took their cue from her,
They sought to follow in her path,
And find their pay in a patient's smile,
Or in a sick one's tender laugh.

The life she lived to many eyes,
May have been concealed from sight,
But to the eyes of the Lord above,
It was a life of humble might.

Her journey now has run its course,
With her work on earth complete,
Today in heaven she takes her place,
At the Master Servant's feet.

There beside heaven's crystal sea,
Where God's servants all are found,
Jesus says, "Well done my child."
As he puts on her servant's crown.

## Where Life Is Young Again

'Tis finished now, the long ordeal,
Of the body's last earthly days.
The painful, speechless time at last,
Gives place to heaven's rays.

'Tis like a storm with chilling wind,
And cold, thick skies of gray,
To near the end of earth's long voyage,
In a helpless kind of way.

But just beyond the final blast,
Of storm's cold, icy wind,
There comes the spring of eternal day,
Where life is young again.

I've shed the robe of flesh I've worn,
Until I've thoroughly worn it out.
Now to me a new robe is given,
The one Christ talked about.

The rooms of earth are left behind,
Which once were dear to me.
Now heaven's mansions before me stand,
Where I'll live for eternity.

And memories sweet of earth's great loves,
Will here with me remain,
Until one by one you each shed earth's robes,
And with me the eternal dwellings gain.

## Each One He Made His Own

He lay down at night in a house on earth,
With a devoted loving wife,
And in the morning in heaven awoke,
With Jesus in never ending life.

It is to you who remain below,
A shock that shakes the earth,
But to his soul that in Jesus dwelt,
The fulfillment of his rebirth.

Now you who in this life have known,
And loved him here below,
Mark well the faith in Jesus he had,
And trace those footsteps as you go.

No one on earth does perfection reach,
Though for it they may strive,
But when in Jesus one does trust,
They will forever be alive.

They'll reign in heaven with the saints,
Who serve the Lion on his throne,
Because the holy Lamb of God,
Has made each one of them his own.

Dr. C.R. Hill, Jr.

## Well Done

A servant of the King has gone,
Home to his Master's house.
Through the fires of life he walked,
As God the flames with grace did douse.

When on his body time worked its curse,
Robbing strength from his every limb;
He leaned the more on Jesus' arms,
And his soul was stronger made by him.

As we watched his earthly features fade,
We saw Jesus likeness become more clear,
In the love and forgiveness that he held,
For all the ones he held so dear.

O' now he walks on streets of gold,
In the pure light of God.
And there he waits for those he loves,
Who still walk on paths of earthly sod.

So shed your tears of sorrow today,
But let each teardrop fall in hope,
Then like him walk on the path of light,
Not letting your soul in darkness grope.

For when that path of Christ he took,
Emerges from earth's refining flame,
Those who keep it faithfully,
Find eternal life in Jesus' name.

## The Garden Gate

We walked with Dad to the garden gate,
From there his path led home to God.
So there for now we bid farewell,
Until we too tread on heaven's sod.

Too soon the garden gate was reached,
So quick the walk with Dad did end,
O' we lingered near the gate a while,
Then he went on to meet our friend.

In our minds we can see them still,
As together they walk toward home.
And though he's gone still we know,
That we're not left here to walk alone.

Our friend who walks Dad home today,
Walks us through this valley low.
Where sorrow assails yet hope prevails,
As now from the garden gate we go.

That hope of course is Jesus Christ,
Who is the resurrection and the life,
He dries our tears at the garden gate,
And makes us victors in life's strife.

Dr. C.R. Hill, Jr.

## An Ode to Valor

A ship went home with tattered sails,
And timbers scraped and worn,
But sailing proud with mast erect,
A victor o'er many a storm.

He's steering now this homeward course,
From the perils he's won escape,
His course he could only chart,
Sailing around the treacherous cape.

With compass chart and morning star,
And his Pilot at the helm,
He's left behind the churning seas,
For his skipper's tranquil realm.

We know men by where they've been,
Or the fortunes they're amassing.
But it's the ripples of the good they do,
That on eternal shores are lasting.

The ripples from the wake he laid,
On his loved one's faces laughing.
And rest assured they'll be seen again,
On distant beaches splashing.

## Beyond the Fields of Brown

It is winter time my love,
I see a different scene.
Fields of brown deprived of snow,
Interspersed with evergreen.

Overhead a turquoise evening sky,
Laced with clouds of pink,
Evokes a certain loneliness,
As the sun begins to sink.

Fields of brown appear drab and drear,
To my summer viewer's eye,
And loneliness seems a thing to fear,
As our day begins to die.

But as my soul attunes to life,
I see beauty in the brown,
And loneliness makes our love more dear
When the sun is going down.

Then in the turquoise evening sky,
My spirit's eye can see,
Beyond the fields in shades of brown,
To God's eternity.

There I see in fields of green,
With endless life anew,
Is your new home with Christ our King,
Where one day I'll join you.

Dr. C.R. Hill, Jr.

## The Runner

As a runner in a marathon,
Yearns for the finish line,
So Benny longed the race he ran,
To cross from the sands of time.

As a mountain climber toils long,
To scale the upward heights;
So Benny toiled each passing day
Until at last he took his flight.

No more he breathes with labor now,
No longer lies he there;
Today he walks the golden streets,
And breathes freely heaven's air.

Though we below may weep today,
For the vacant chair he leaves,
Friends above rejoice anew,
And Benny no longer grieves.

We often note the youth in stride,
Who runs for an earthly prize,
But Benny ran in a nobler race,
For a crown beyond the skies.

## The Priceless Jewel

A Jewel has fallen from earth's crown,
And passed beyond our midst.
For she now adorns the heavenly courts,
Because life's goal she did not miss.

A sister she of loving care,
Who always sought to lead the way,
A loving wife and doting aunt,
Who looked to Jesus every day.

Her years on earth three score and ten,
Then God added sixteen more,
For her to grace the family crown,
And point to Heaven's Door.

Now she has gone to find her rest,
For the body soon gives out,
Yet only then does one really live,
Who trusted Jesus with no doubt.

For he is the life of every soul,
Whose shadow falls upon the earth,
And to all who will his gift receive,
He gives for eternal life a birth.

# Flying

"Hey, Dad,
Can I go fly with you?
I want to see the moon up close,
From the cockpit's cloudless view."

"Sure Son,
I'm always glad for you to come along.
The sky is clear and the moon is full.
Together we'll watch it rise 'fore long."

"Up here,
My soul feels that it is free,
And among my fondest joys Son,
Is you sharing flight with me."

"Look Dad,
The moon is rising now!
Dad, up here I feel so close to you,
You think we could touch the moon somehow?"

Well Son,
The moon is a little out of reach,
For the humble wings of man,
But spread your spirit's eagle wings,
And touch the heavens with your hand."

## Around the Upward Bend

Though in a moment's twinkling eye,
Our mortal life may end,
It does not mean the journey's over,
But the road's made an upward bend.

And though the turn does for a while,
Take us from our loved one's side,
It does not mean all hope is gone,
Or that the love we shared has died.

For life on earth's a fleeting thing,
And each must round this bend,
From whence the road continues on,
Until it draws loved ones near again.

So don't despair though now you grieve,
For the one you loved who is gone,
In God's time you will reunite,
Where life and love go on.

Dr. C.R. Hill, Jr.

## Life at Road's End

The way through life can be a joyful road,
If its traveler there walks with the Lord.
If love is the force that carries one along,
And their day is lighted by God's word.

Yet as great as it is, it is only a road;
It is not an end in itself.
It is meant to lead to a heavenly home,
Not a path leading to earthly wealth.

Such was the road our dear one has walked,
Along it her Jesus she'd known.
Now as her ashes are laid here to rest,
We know that today in heaven she is home.

Still our road of life goes on from here,
Through a future to us yet unseen,
But of this as we travel we can be sure,
That Jesus will our journey redeem.

So walk from today in assurance of grace,
Embraced in his love be secure.
When you walk with him whatever may come,
Your life too at road's end will endure.

## The Anchors of God's Grace

Like a raging hurricane,
The storm of death has come,
To take your loved one from your midst,
Her course of life now run.

Now the rocks along life's shore,
Threaten your life also to undo,
With doubt, despair and disbelief,
How will you ever make it through?

Here are some anchors for your soul,
That will help you to endure life's storm.
Hold fast to them in this dark night,
And pray for God's new day to dawn.

For God is with you in these waves,
His provision holds you secure.
His pardon rebukes the winds of sin.
Forever will his love endure.

Be assured that as it is for you,
Also for Carol these anchors do apply.
In his love Jesus took her by the hand,
And walked her home no more to die.

Dr. C.R. Hill, Jr.

## The Homeland of the Soul

Another soul has traveled home,
Not to his native land of earth,
But to that homeland of the soul,
Gained by in Christ a second birth.

His journey here was rich and full,
With an eye for simple beauty,
From his heart flowed values noble,
Like love, and truth, and duty.

He'd know the sorrows oppressions bring,
He once had without a homeland been,
Thus all the more he rejoiced in heart,
As on native soil he was walking once again.

Yet his heart resided elsewhere too,
In his adopted homelands free,
It was there he met his lifelong love,
And here they raised their family.

Yet the souls that fill these jars of clay,
Are never fully at home on earthly sod,
There is a deeper yearning within,
That seeks our eternal home with God.

So now our loved one has journeyed on,
Not to his native land on earth,
But to that homeland of the soul,
He gained by in Christ his second birth.

## The Music of His Life

The music of his hands,
Would lift our voices up in song,
And lighten up the loads,
Of our weary days so long.

The music of heart,
Was filled with friendship sweet,
Making better persons,
Of those he chanced to meet.

The music of his work,
Contained a healing balm,
Delivering many folks from illnesses,
While their anxious fears he'd calm.

Yes the music of his life,
Shall still echo through these hills,
For as we recall him fondly,
It yet our hearts with joy fills.

O' the music of his faith,
Our courage did inspire,
As hand and hand with Jesus,
He walked faithfully through life's fire.

Dr. C.R. Hill, Jr.

## The Angel to Us Loaned

With golden slippers on her feet,
She dances down the crystal way,
For she woke today in Jesus' arms,
In her home of eternal day.

No tubes she wears to help her breath,
Her food, The Bread of Life.
She rose this morning from this land,
Where her body knew such strife.

Yet while she was with us down here,
She let not strife possess her soul.
Rather by God's grace she used the strife,
To point us all towards heaven's goal.

She taught us how to love each other,
And to cherish every child.
She taught us how to hold God's hand,
When our ride through life gets wild.

She showed us all to cherish,
Every moment in time we're given.
And to become like Jesus more each day,
Is the real reason for our livin.

So, Lord Jesus we thank you now,
For lending to us your angle fair.
We are placing her back into your arms,
Assured one day we'll join her there.

## A Saint Has Transferred Home

A saint transferred from here to home,
At the end of a long and fruitful day,
She long ago had made her plans
To walk the Master's cross-led way.

Her loved ones here sad to see her go,
Nonetheless have joy within,
For her long ordeal on earth is o'er,
And in heaven they'll meet her again.

A mother blessed so long on earth,
Is double blessed indeed,
To live to see her children grown,
And to watch them all succeed.

So you my friends gathered here today,
Have little cause to stand and grieve,
Go rejoice in her length of days,
And that God does now her soul receive.

Then fix your gaze not on this plot below,
But on God's yonder mountain high,
And let your spirit soar with God,
Until you with Jesus walk the sky.

# The Harbor of God's Arms

Another soul went sailing out,
To join the Lord today,
A soul that near perfection reached,
As he walked this earth's pathway.

'Tis strange the way the sands of life,
Like grit against the soul,
Can rub upon the human heart,
Till it shines like precious gold.

It was the case in this one's life,
As hardship and struggle came,
It only made him cling the more,
To his hope in Jesus' name.

As the twilight gathered 'round,
And earth's day drew to its end,
I saw a broad smile cross his face,
Then he set out to greet his friend.

That friend with whom he'd often sailed,
Over earth's seas of raging storms,
Would pilot now his ship eternal,
To the harbor of God's arms.

## The Crossing

I met her there on Jordan's bank,
Where I took her by the hand,
We talked for just a little while,
As she gazed on Canaan's land.

A weary traveler she'd come to be,
Yet with a ready wit and mind,
'Twas not on life she's given up,
But to heaven she had resigned.

She loved her family she was to leave,
Far too much to weigh them down,
So she was ready for that brighter home,
And her heavenly robe and crown.

O' she lingered only briefly there,
Then released this hand of mine,
And taking hold of Jesus' hand,
She crossed from earth and time.

Dr. C.R. Hill, Jr.

## In God's Eternal Book

Another saint has gone home today,
As heaven's ranks have grown.
Though your hearts are heavy now,
You will not walk through life alone.

She walked with you the may miles,
That filled her earthly years,
She shared with you the happy times,
And helped to dry your tears.

Today her journey is ended here,
She now walks on heaven's shore.
She looks with joy on Jesus' face,
And on the loved ones gone before.

Now you who still remain behind,
Hold fast the path she took,
Till you like she shall hear your name,
Read from God's eternal book.

## From the Top of the Hill

I'll take my leave to the top of the hill,
From whence I can look back o'er my life,
Then, I'll look ahead to that heavenly realm,
Where awaits my new home and my wife.

Oh, I've tarried long in this tent here below,
In the main life's been good and I blessed,
But my cup is now full and my years have run out,
And it is time I move on to my rest.

You'll miss me I know and it is alright to grieve,
For the bond that's between us has been strong,
So weep for a spell then get on with your life,
And we will meet up in heaven before long.

I've now caught the view from the top of the hill,
Heaven's beauty before me I now see,
The glory exceeds all on earth I had dreamed,
And best of all, here comes Jesus for me.

## It Is Finished

"It is finished." Jesus whispered,
As he closed his eyes in death.
Into his Father's waiting hands,
His spirit flew with parting breath.

"It is finished. Jesus whispered,
His course in life complete,
And with his parting words in life,
Death and hell are in defeat.

"It is finished." Jesus whispered,
Man's debt of sin is paid.
For with his parting drops of blood,
The full payment he had made.

"It is finished." Jesus whispers,
Now to the souls whose course is run,
And hand-in-hand he gently leads them,
Into the life his death has won!

## On the Death of a Teacher

A teacher dear has crossed the bar,
Stepped beyond the veil of time.
Her earthly form and worldly gain,
With quiet grace resigned.

Earthly form is of fading worth,
We, too, must soon return to dust;
What counts is what's within the heart,
And that on Christ one trusts.

Her heart was tired from time and toil,
Her steps had grown less sure,
But straight and tall through heaven's gates,
Her spirit soars secure.

We shed out tears of selfish grief,
For a friend has bid farewell.
But she has entered her eternal home,
In glory no tongue can tell.

So let us follow the path she made,
This woman with a teacher's heart,
Until once again we see her face,
Where we never more shall part.

# A Giant I Recall

I remember hauling hay,
From the field before the rain.
I remember sitting by the TV,
To watch a baseball game.

I remember eating fried turtle,
At Granny Brown's one summer night,
How I just couldn't get that turtle,
In the pond quite out of sight.

I remember churning ice cream,
Sitting around out in the yard.
I remember how old Jip would run,
To church behind the car.

It is the little things I now recall,
Nothing really so great and grand,
Except in all those little things of life,
He'd like a giant always stand.

He'd seen the fires of death up close,
He'd served his country in the Guard.
I don't recall one complaining word.
He played as dealt life's every card.

There is another thing,
That always comes to mind,
It is the love he had for others,
And how life to Jesus he had resigned.

## Her Songs Will Keep On Ringing

Another ship set out today,
Without a moment's warning,
She came to sing her praise to God,
But left with him this morning.

Her leaving took us all by storm,
As we watched her sails departing.
It seemed her stay was just begun,
Her music only starting.

But her captain called and she obeyed,
In the way she was accustomed.
With all she did while on our shore,
She showed us how to trust him.

So though we'll miss her as we go,
Her songs will keep on ringing.
And rest assured our faith in God,
That in heaven's choir she's singing.

Dr. C.R. Hill, Jr.

## The Quiet Man and Heaven's Son

A quiet man went home this week,
He left with Sunday's dawn.
O' he tarried long on earth with us,
Now to heaven he has gone.

Throughout his life he first of all,
Sought what he knew was just.
Kindness was his trademark too,
As he walked with God in trust.

His spirit aspired to noble heights,
For the people of our town
By generous deeds he'd lift folks up,
When life would knock them down.

His true and faithful loyalty,
Spoke more than words convey,
Of a character formed by Christ,
And strengthened day by day.

As does for all, his time ran out,
Now his race on earth he's run.
Today he strolls on streets of gold,
This quiet man and heaven's Son.

## Across the Finish Line

How swiftly now life's race was run,
How quick her course behind.
Each hurdle cleared stood in review,
As she crossed life's finish line.

Her race began with strong desire,
And dreams of serving those in need.
Her race then ran with faithful care,
And love attending every deed.

Each hurdle loomed with imposing height,
As she approached it in her stride,
And each was cleared by strength and grace,
With Jesus running at her side.

Then in that final stretch of track,
With her own strength fully spent,
She crossed the finish in victorious joy,
By the strength her Savior sent.

Dr. C.R. Hill, Jr.

## The Teacher and the Saint

She was to all of us a saint,
The teacher of our way,
Now she moves beyond this earth,
Having shed her tent of clay.

It was for her the natural thing,
Having loved all she knew on earth,
And having traced the lives of those,
Who had gone before her birth.

Now with them on heaven's shore,
Bathed in eternal light,
She walks with Jesus by her side,
By his resurrection's might.

She leaves with us her legacy,
As a teacher, mother, friend,
Who loved the time she spent with us,
And showed us how in life to win.

By placing all your faith in Christ,
And living each and every day,
By following as best you can,
Jesus as the one true way.

## From the Topside Down

He viewed the world from a lofty perch,
As he worked high above the ground,
For a man with the roofer's trade,
Sees man's work from topside down.

Most people tend to go through life,
With a "seen from bottom" view,
That affects the way they value things,
As well as what they say and do.

Seen through the eyes of such a view,
A gruff and rugged man he'd be,
But such a view would never reveal,
The man in him I learned to see.

The bottom view was not the one,
By which he chose to mold himself,
He from the topside down did choose,
To build his character of wealth.

Ah, when one lives from topside down,
'Tis from Jesus they take life's cue,
They let God's lofty thoughts and ways,
Shape what they value, and hold true.

So you who grieve may dry your eyes,
Today he looks from the topside down,
For he has climbed God's ladder of life,
Now on the topside, he wears his crown.

# From Papa's Cotton Basket

When she was but a wee child,
With her Papa in the field,
He'd put her in a cotton basket,
While he the soil tilled.

Safe beneath a shade tree,
She would the hours spend,
Until her Papa finished working,
And they'd walk home again.

In time she met our Papa,
'Twas not long Until they were wed.
And for all the years that followed,
They lived out the vows they said.

Through the years they labored,
She and Papa side by side,
They found their joy in family,
In each child they took their pride.

Then Papa went home with Jesus,
While she waited in the shade alone,
Until on their mansion he finished working,
Now together they've walked home.

## Beholding God's Eternal Dawn

The time that comes for every soul,
Has here your loved one claimed,
And he has taken his journey now,
To God for whom we all are named.

While this leaves an empty place,
In the heart of each of you,
It also creates more room within,
For the Christ who walks with you.

It is Jesus who has created us,
To his perfect image bear,
And life on earth a journey is,
On which we for that end prepare.

When the journey's end is reached,
And any perfection yet we lack,
It is the grace of Jesus Christ,
That in heaven has our back.

For by his death upon the cross,
And his resurrection from the grave,
He paid the price for all our sins,
As to us eternal life he gave.

So weep a moment here today,
For your loved one from you gone,
But then let joy fill your hearts,
For he has entered God's eternal dawn.

Dr. C.R. Hill, Jr.

# With Heaven's Path Conformed

There is for each of us a path through life,
That leads to heaven's way.
The task we each must in life complete,
Is to merge our path with God's each day.

When our journey's end we reach,
We then will on to heaven go,
If along our path through life,
We did come to Jesus know.

O' our loved one here today,
To God's pathway did adhere.
And ever closer with Jesus walked,
As her journey's end drew near.

Now we have gathered in this place,
On this sacred hallowed ground,
To send her off with words of praise,
As she receives her eternal crown.

You will surely shed some tears,
For sorrow now fills your heart,
Yet be assured you'll see her again,
If from God's path you not depart.

So as you journey from this day,
See that your path with his conforms,
And when your journey's end you reach,
He'll bear you home in loving arms.

## To A 'Homegoing' Queen

A champion has arrived at home,
Her victory finally won.
She ran her race through refining fire,
Fully confident in God's Son.

The pains and fears of Satan's power,
Sought in vain to rob her peace,
For by the power of Jesus Christ,
Her faith and hope just would not cease.

Nor could pain her joy dispel,
No matter how it did try,
Despair was never a choice for her,
For she did fully on God rely.

She didn't expect death not to come,
To claim her tent of clay,
Rather far beyond all doubt she knew,
After death dawns God's new day.

Oh, it saddened her to leave us here,
Yet she knew it is for just a while.
For in a moment of eternal time,
She will greet us with a smile.

So for now we who remain behind,
Are grieved that she is gone,
Yet through the faith she revealed to us,
We shall her memory carry on.

As we ourselves our journey make,
With trust in God's great love,
We'll strive as she through Jesus Christ,
To join her at God's throne above.

Dr. C.R. Hill, Jr.

## At Home Where the Angel Sings

Mother left for home today,
She rose on morning wings,
To leave behind the world of sorrows,
For the one where the angel sings.

O how her leaving takes us by storm,
For she has so suddenly from us flown,
Yet we will still in our Savior trust,
Knowing she is in her heavenly home.

And from the path that leads to life,
We can still hear her call so soft,
"Continue on in faith, hope, and love,"
Until you too take up your home aloft."

So though our hearts are heavy now,
And this way below seems dim,
We'll trust in Jesus to walk with us,
For we know above she walks with him.

Yea, in the comfort that Jesus brings,
We'll pick up our life and carry on,
Assured by the grace of Christ our Lord,
Mother now joins heaven's chorus in song.

## As the Eagle's Strength Renew

When time has taken the Eagle's strength,
And his talons have grown too long.
When his beak has grown too crooked to eat,
And the power for his wings is gone.

When all these things have befallen him,
He does not die like others do,
But on a mountain high he takes retreat,
And there he does his strength renew.

Like an Eagle does renew his strength,
Are they who wait upon the Lord.
To no earthly mountain do they retreat,
But the one across old Jordan's ford.

It was from Lynn time had stolen strength,
Until with us he could no longer stay,
So to God's mountain he has taken flight,
With Jesus showing him the way.

His strength renewed in heaven now,
Like on feet with wings he walks.
Now in the light of God's dear Son,
Today with the saints he talks.

And in the house that God prepared,
For him with Christ to dwell,
He would send us greetings saying,
"Weep not for me, now all is well."

Dr. C.R. Hill, Jr.

## Beyond the Forest Dark

In a woods dark and wild,
A child of mine did lose his way.
In the maze of tangled paths,
He got fully lost one day.

No fault it was of his own,
That in those woods he'd gone,
It was the forest of his birth,
There he'd lived his whole life long.

Yet on that day the tangled maze,
Of shadowy paths unclear,
Did obscure the trail he knew,
Causing him to wrongly steer.

I the Lord did find him there,
Too far from home he'd strayed,
So I took him to the home,
That for him my death had made.

I know the heartbreak that you feel,
Over this your tragic loss;
It is the same feeling that I have,
Over each one who rejects my cross.

But those in life who once receive,
My gift of love and grace,
I never shall from my book of life,
Their eternal name erase.

Now in the forest of your grief,
You feel you can go on no longer;
Yet by my grace you will emerge,
And in my service be the stronger.

44

## Gone to Be with God

An ordinary man today,
Has gone to be with God.
His body will now lie sleeping,
Here beneath his native sod.

Yet today in heaven,
His soul is wide awake,
For while living here among us,
He did the hand of Jesus take.

Then with his Savior right beside him,
He did walk earth's final miles,
Until he crossed Jordan's chilly waters,
To his home on Heaven's Golden Isles.

O' we'll miss him here among us,
As our journeys we complete,
But we will in Heaven be reunited,
When we cast our crowns at Jesus' feet.

Until then let us keep on trusting,
In the Lord of Life above,
While we spend our earthly hours,
Beneath the wings of God's great love.

Dr. C.R. Hill, Jr.

# Like the Master Archer's Arrow

When a brother who has shared our years,
From earth is called to go,
It brings yet closer still the thought,
That our time is short down here below.

One finds themselves then looking back,
Over what in life they've done,
What is the mark they've left behind,
What kind of race they've run.

So now it is with our brother dear,
Whom God has summoned home,
As we pause to count the blessing,
That in life we him have known.

We reflect upon the kind of man,
That through Christ he came to be,
The values that his character shaped,
Until we could Jesus in him see.

O' may we each now lift our gaze,
From looking back let us look ahead,
Then set more firmly the heavenly goal,
For when our last words on earth are said.

Jesus calls us each to chose,
Between the broad way and the narrow,
And by his grace to hit the mark,
Like the master archer's arrow.

So now the time has come to bid farewell,
To our brother we here have known,
Yet we in Christ shall greet him anew,
When we too from earth have flown.

## Lady Jane

Tall she stood and straight,
Not in frame alone,
'Twas in character and in grace,
That she to us by "Lady Jane" was known.

Character and grace that sprang
From an inner sense of worth,
For she in Christ her Lord,
Had known the meaning of rebirth.

Royal yes,
A true child of God her king,
As with the nature of his Son,
Her life did with every fiber ring.

O how the shadow that she cast,
Did the lives of others lift,
As they sought to reach God's high ground,
By receiving his salvation's gift.

Still her firm but gentle touch,
Is by those who felt it on their life,
Yet giving guidance for their way,
As it brings them comfort in their strife.

On streets of purer gold,
She now walks today,
With friends and loved ones who like her,
Traveled God's straight and narrow way.

# In Heaven's Mansion Grand

Mother left for home today,
On a springtime morning breeze.
Her lingering years now at their full,
She crossed the bar with ease.

She felt at home where Dad had been,
In the house they both had shared.
O she'd be content with nothing else,
Till in the home that Christ prepared.

To heaven's shores she now has flown,
Beyond all her earthly pains and fears.
There Fannie, George, and Paul await,
To wipe away her earthly tears.

Together in the joy of heaven's day,
She with the gathered saints now sings,
And prays that each of you may know,
The gentle peace that Jesus brings.

So lift your hearts with heaven's hope,
And by your faith in Christ be glad,
For Jesus has built a mansion grand,
Where now live your Mom and Dad.

## The Keel That Keeps Us True

Some men stand like towering masts,
Whose yardarms hold the sail,
While others, like deep running keels,
Hold ships steady through the gale,

When Jesus taught the way of truth,
And the things that win life's seal,
He said the ones who were truly great,
Would resemble more the keel.

The stately mast is always seen,
Towering above the ship of state,
But beneath the surface hid from view,
It is the keel that keeps her straight.

'Tis such a man we honor now,
As we pause to bid adieu.
Paul Cates, a man whose life lived right,
Was like the keel that keeps us true.

Farewell, dear friend and true companion,
Who in life did your good out of sight.
Go rejoice in heaven's inversions,
Where the keel is appraised as upright.

Dr. C.R. Hill, Jr.

## By Nature's Ancient Bridge

O glorious morning bright and fair
   With autumn's early chill.
O mountains clothed in autumn's robes
   To give the soul a thrill.

'Twas such a morning she rose to greet,
   With her warm and gentle grin.
She'd fill her cup of life each day,
   Till it would overflow the brim.

She'd catch the bus whenever she could,
   To some delightful distant place,
And warm the hearts of all on board,
   With her glad and quiet grace.

She loved to share the ride with friends,
   She loved to laugh over every meal.
She lived to share the sights with them,
   And their joy in turn to feel.

How true it was that she lived to see,
   All the wonders of God's hand,
And so it was she had come with us,
   In that ancient place to stand.

'Twas there by nature's ancient bridge,
   Where presidents did once roam,
She stepped across to heaven's shores,
   And with Jesus she walked home.

## She Danced Into Heaven with a Smile

With a lilt in her step and a song on her lips,
She made ready an adventure to start,
Off on a journey new discoveries to make,
She was traveling with God in her heart.

A child full of life, and a fountain of love,
With compassion for persons left out,
A dancer and swimmer in awe of the sea,
She was growing up in her life as a scout.

Through Christmas love she learned how to give,
Until wishing she like Jesus could be,
Would when finished with earth's passing glance,
Give her eyes –so another could see.

She set out from home and family she loved,
For new vistas of life to explore.
Only God knew the turn her path would take,
That would bring her that day to his door.

Saddened I'm sure to leave loved ones behind,
Knowing they would see her on earth not again,
Yet with a lilt in her step, and a song on her lips,
She did her adventure in heaven begin.

With her mom and dad and her brother too,
She did travel that day for a while,
Then she went with Jesus the rest of her trip,
And danced into heaven with a smile.

## The Summit Reached

I've seen cyclists climb high mountain passes,
And hikers on a steep mountain trail,
Yet those who the greatest heights have reached,
Were they who the paths of heaven did scale.

Just such a climber our sister was,
With God's sure word her hiking staff.
At challenges that would turn the weaker back,
She would with confident faith just laugh.

With kind and caring hands she served.
With skill and knowledge she did teach;
As she sought at every turn in life,
To help other climbers heaven reach.

The summit of her climb achieved,
She took from us her earthly leave,
And with the Master Climber she went,
To her crown of life receive.

Now you who climbed this earthly trail,
With her the longest way,
Will in her footsteps yet climb on,
Until you rejoin her in God's eternal day.

## Evening's Homeward Call

I saw a child in a yard at play,
With friends in the evening's glow,
When someone called from a kitchen door,
And she arose from play to go.

O, how like life this simple scene,
Of children in a yard at play,
Then the call, "Come home now child",
And we arise to close life's day.

How soon it seems some evenings come,
As life on earth us doeth consume.
Then before we know, it's time to leave,
And take up life in our heavenly room.

'Tis then we know that life on earth,
Is measured not in length of days,
But by faith and hope and the love we have,
And how by these we shape our ways.

For when by these we've sought to live,
And leaned each night upon God's grace,
Then we've naught but praise to give,
When at evening's call we behold God's face.

Dr. C.R. Hill, Jr.

## In the Memory of Her Love

Some say she is not among us,
That she has gone to heaven above,
Yet her presence lingers after,
In the memory of her love.

She was here so full of living,
In the joy of her youth,
And she bubbled with the gladness,
Of God's gracious love and truth.

She had aimed her life at giving,
Aid and comfort to the ill,
Then the nurse became the patient,
Who though sick was giving still.

To her son and precious husband,
She wanted more than love to give,
That with her in heaven's mansion,
They may in time forever live.

Though for now she is not among us,
Her face and form now passed from view,
Still her presence watches over,
And she will always walk with you.

## The Graduate

He graduated Sunday noon,
From earth's university of clay.
The lessons of a lifetime learned,
He now embarks upon eternal day.

He walked through life in Jesus' shoes,
Until they were well worn and broken in,
Now he walks the streets of gold,
With Jesus Christ his life-long friend.

His place on earth is vacant now,
His rocker on the porch is still,
For today he views a grander lake,
Than that one nestled in the hills.

O' I imagine on heaven's shores,
He yet today is holding court,
Reciting poems and swapping yarns,
With some player of his favorite sport.

Yet heaven is not just a resting place,
Where no worthwhile work is done.
There this life's lessons are employed,
In the perfect service of God's Son.

So in that grander vineyard high,
He joyfully tills and tends the vines,
Where grow the fruits of life eternal,
That feed our human souls, and minds.

## In The House His Love Designed

She talked with him three times a day,
And often in between.
He was always present at her side,
Though by others there unseen.

The friendship that they shared,
Was her source of life and hope,
Through many trials and tribulations,
It was the source of her power to cope.

When with this friend in conversation,
She would speak out loud,
The beauty of words she chose,
Would drive away the darkest cloud.

But alas with time she did grow weary,
Of these long distance talks,
Where none but her could see her friend,
Nor she with him take her evening walks.

O' there comes a time in friendships,
When neither friend can yet abide,
Any amount of further separation,
They must be fully at each other's side.

So with cup of life now overflowing,
With her character as gold refined,
She went home to live with Jesus,
In the house his love for her designed.

## A Lady Following Jesus

I bid her my farewell,
The day before the fact,
She assured me she was ready,
Though I had no doubt of that.

I'd come to love and to admire her,
As a lady through and through.
I put great value in her wisdom;
I knew her perceptions to be true.

I admired her quiet dignity,
And the way she truth discerned,
Her laughter was like music,
She was truly one from whom to learn.

She told me she had packed her suitcase,
About a quarter century past,
Then she lived life's every minute,
Right until the very last.

I knew her walk with God was constant,
I could tell she awoke to him each day.
I saw her stay ever in his presence,
Through the pain that plagued her way.

Now this lady has followed Jesus,
Into death's dark and awful cave,
But she had no fear at her life's ending,
She trusted Jesus' triumph o'er the grave.

Dr. C.R. Hill, Jr.

# Fast in the Master's Hand

A young ship torn by sudden wind,
Has thus put out to sea.
A squall has loosed her moorings to earth,
And set her sail for eternity.

But not to fear; she is not lost,
Though she's sailed beyond our sight.
Her sails now catch the Master's breeze,
As on she steers into His light.

And we who linger here behind,
Still moored on earth's sad shore,
Will one day loose our ropes of flesh,
And be joined with her once more.

When comes the time for us to sail,
Whether on breezes or fierce storms,
We, too, will cross the eternal sea,
Borne safely in Jesus' arms.

Then in the light of eternal day,
We'll greet her in that land,
And evermore securely dwell,
Held fast in the Master's hand.

## When the Heart Will Sing and Dance

There is a path for each to take,
In this journey we call life,
For some it's short for some it's long,
For all some joy and some strife.

'Tis not how steep the climb,
Or through what pleasant vales it winds,
'Tis how one grows along the way,
That the soul refines.

So it is her path complete,
Her journey on earth now ended,
She takes now the upward course,
With the Savior she befriended.

New paths above she treads today,
And these streets are paved with gold.
For Jesus has her life redeemed,
Now heaven's treasures to her unfold.

For sure the eyes that loved her here,
Are misty yet with tears,
As now is ended for a time,
Her company through the years.

But in a twinkling of an eye,
It will seem at backward glance,
You'll be reunited at God's throne,
Then your hearts will sing and dance.

## Salute to a Quiet Man

Alas, Charlie Coan has put out to sea,
His spirit bound is now set free.

While he on earth his simple style,
Embraced what matters most, like a friendly smile.

Or children's laughter from the back yard swing,
And the beauty found in a common thing.

A servant too whose steady pace,
Leaves town and world a better place.

He parted much as his life was spent,
With quiet grace he calmly went.

No dread had he of what lay beyond,
He went to greet the day that is before the dawn.

Dressed in robes of Christ this quiet man,
In faith reached up and grasped God's hand.

## Birch Cook's Store

His store was west of town,
Unless by town you meant the one west of him, then east.
Several miles either way.
A country store was what his had always been.
In the country.

Why two – three years ago,
We hunted on his land across the road.
There is a church there now,
And houses where then only briars would grow.

Burch was usually there,
When I would happen to stop in.
He was famous for his burgers; I enjoyed his iced tea.
He would be seated at a table,
And there we would visit friend to friend.
That was his major role.

The store just made the place,
For the community to gather 'round,
Where young and old could interact,
And one could always find a friendly face.

The country is changing now.
And with its passing there is a sadness.
But the fact we've known such a place at all,
With this unpretentious backstage man,
Is a source of strength and gladness.

Dr. C.R. Hill, Jr.

## Off Again

She'd make a friend then plan a trip,
And off she would go for a while.
Everywhere she greeted folks,
She left them with a smile.

When other hearts were scared to move,
Being uncertain about the morrow,
She didn't let it bother her,
For she feared not the threat of sorrow.

She came of age in troubled times,
Prepared to take on the world alone,
Then she found her life-long mate,
And together they made their home.

Then when his race on earth was run,
She saw no cause to fold her tent,
She drew upon her inner strength,
Then off again she went.

With Christ her friend she'd planed a trip,
Now they've headed off on it in style.
But by and by on heaven's shore,
She will greet you with her smile.

## When Came Her Crossing Time

When heaven's time for crossing came,
And your mother started home,
No fear there was at water's edge,
For she did not have to cross alone.

The hand she held as she stepped out,
Was no stranger to that sea,
He'd crossed once for every soul,
So all could live eternally.

Though your mother's eyes have closed,
To earthly sights and view,
They are opened wide to heaven's scenes,
Where God makes all things new.

Now in a robe as white as light,
With Christ she walks up streets of gold,
To the mansion he has built for her,
Where we shall never more grow old.

There to meet her at the door,
Are the loved ones she knew here,
As God welcomes her with open arms,
Then wipes away each earthly tear.

Dr. C.R. Hill, Jr.

## In The Light That Christmas Brings

If death and darkness were all there was,
When life is finished here,
Then all the years we spend on earth,
Would be spent in dread and fear.

But into our darkness God sends his light,
In the birth of his dear Son,
And we know from him when finished here,
Our real life has just begun.

So it was before Christmas Eve,
Jerry's life with us was through.
God has called him home with Christ,
Ahead of me and you.

And while our hearts are sad today,
Because from us he now is gone,
We know because of Christmas Day,
Jerry in heaven today lives on.

Our days on earth can feel very long,
When those we've loved must leave,
But on the face of heaven's clock,
It is quite short the time we grieve.

So shed your tears of sorrow today,
They are the tribute love demands,
But weep them in the assurance that,
They will be dried by God's own hands.

## Evening Time At Home

Another soul has at evening come,
By the way that Christ made known,
O'er the treacherous course of life,
To safely arrive at home.

As every soul that is born to life,
Is cast upon the sands of time,
And there must choose their goal,
Whether earth or life sublime.

Oh it was settled soon for him,
For he chose the path of life.
He lived by what the way required,
Like a faithful husband to a wife.

Yes, a quiet man of dignity,
Who in all his deeds was true,
One trusting in that grace divine,
That rescues me and you.

So it is this Pilgrim has come,
By the way that Christ made known,
Across the shifting sands of time,
To reach at evening time his home.

Dr. C.R. Hill, Jr.

## On the Wings of Fluid Grace

I watched a hawk fly across my path,
Then land on a streamside limb.
He moved with such a fluid grace,
That it made me envy him.

A pair of bluebirds later came,
To rest on the back deck perch,
As I sat with her and thought of how,
I have known these two in church.

A braver man I have never known,
Each step to this life's end,
He bore his pain with unshaken grace,
For he knew Jesus friend to friend.

That hawk I saw fly across my path,
I really think 'twas him,
Telling me he was free at last,
To move about with grace again.

Yes, and in a greater realm of space,
Than can earth at best afford,
With grace he flies to heaven's door,
In the freedom of his Lord.

Now for this pair I've known in church,
She does not fly on from here alone,
For Jesus Christ flies on her wing,
As George looks on from heaven's home.

## In You Her Song Lives On

There is a house not made with hands,
That awaits beyond the sky,
A home God has prepared for us,
When from life on earth we die.

Though mortal life be dear and sweet,
It for all must someday end,
But when it does by God's great grace,
We do in heaven have a friend.

Yes, Jesus Christ gave his life for us,
That we may forever with him live.
And when death takes a loved one dear,
He does to us his comfort give.

Today you mourn the one you loved,
Who has so quickly from you flown,
But she lives on beyond the sky,
And in the love to you she's shown.

So weep for now, and shed your tears,
Then arise and by faith be strong.
O' let her love live on in you,
And your life will sing her song.

Dr. C.R. Hill, Jr.

## With Jesus I've Gone Fishing

Daddy I've gone fishing,
That was my evening plan,
Now I am fishing in new waters,
Fishing with the Son of Man.

Mom and Dad I want to thank you,
For all the love you showed to me,
Now please don't worry any,
I am at home with Jack and Rea.

The family is up here waiting,
Gathered all around God's throne,
They are waiting for the time to come,
When the rest of you've come home.

Mom, I know the way is hard for you,
I know your heart just wants to break,
But Jesus is walking right beside you,
And your hand he wants to take.

Oh Daddy let me tell you,
About heaven's bright crystal sea,
Some day I want to see you,
Fishing out on this lake with me.

Well now everybody, here comes Peter,
James and John and Andrew too,
With them and Jesus I'll be fishing,
For the heart of each of you.

# If for a Moment One Believes

A dying thief upon a cross,
A life full of sin's regret,
Did in sorrow to Jesus turn,
And found that God did love him yet.

Onlooking crowds could not believe,
That God could receive one such as he,
His life had nothing but a problem been,
Now could he hope to heaven see?

Yet entry into heaven's gate,
Is not a thing that one can earn,
But is freely given by God's grace,
When one in sorrow does to Jesus turn.

Thus even a troubled soul from earth,
With even a whisper does repent,
A life once lost on sin's dark path,
Is raised above from death's descent.

We have always much to mourn,
When a kinsman from us leaves,
But life eternal is God's great gift,
If one but for a moment believes.

Dr. C.R. Hill, Jr.

# The Gates of Heaven Gained

Let me tell you about a man I know,
Who changed my life my friend,
I've had peace deep in my soul,
Since by faith I let him in.

An orphan was I at sea adrift,
Like Moses among the reeds,
Until he appointed a caring home,
To love and meet my needs.

Yet I recoiled from his hand,
I sought to live my life my way,
So he sent me a loving wife,
To show me heaven's lighted day.

Through her love he wore me down,
Until I could resist his grace no more,
So I gave heed to his tireless knock,
And opened my heart's door.

I tell you friend the change he brought,
Set my feet on heaven's road,
For when I allowed him in my heart,
He relieved my sinful load.

Ah, my loving bride is long now gone,
Yet the love I learned from her remains,
For by its light I met Jesus Christ,
Now the gates of heaven I've gained.

## Heaven's Gain

A lovely lady today set sail,
With the morning's rising sun,
And the honor roll of heaven's saints,
Was increased today by one.

We saw her last on Tuesday-noon,
With her customary smile.
To church she came to lunch with friends,
In her customary style.

Who of us was dreaming then,
That before a new day's dawn,
We would lose a trusted friend,
And this lovely lady would be gone.

Though her parting leaves you stunned,
And wondering what to do;
She would bid you not to grieve,
That her work on earth was through.

Well she taught things that count,
In totaling up life's sum,
She's now gone home to be with God,
And wear the crown she's won.

So firm you'll stand in family love –
Holding fast God's hand of grace,
And rest assured that in heaven's home,
You will see again her face.

Dr. C.R. Hill, Jr.

## In Strength She Now Is Dancing

It took a special kind of lady,
To be this preacher's wife,
Her husband answered to a call,
That altered her whole life.

She seldom had a choice,
Of the life that she would live,
As to a congregation,
Her husband she would give.

Nor could she very easily,
Her own person be,
As there were many expectations,
Of what the church wished in her to see.

Yet she was by God anointed,
To stand by her husband's side,
Empowered by God's Spirit,
For her life's victorious ride.

Now her journey here has ended,
To a new appointment she has gone,
Not to a parsonage, but a mansion,
Where joyous life goes on and on.

Here she carried heavy burdens,
In her body made weak by time;
Now she in strength is dancing,
For Jesus her gold here did refine.

## An Amplifying Echo

I heard an echo ringing clear,
From the canyon walls of time,
The clarion voice of one who now,
Walks along the hills sublime.

The power of his resonant voice,
The shadow of his soul,
Still fall upon the ear and heart,
Bending wills to God's control.

Though we still long for face and form,
In a being we can touch,
'Tis the amplifying echo now,
That around the world is doing much.

For while one lives upon this earth,
They are bound by time and place,
But the shadow of a saintly life,
Inspires hearts throughout the race.

Dr. C.R. Hill, Jr.

## A Man from Heaven Sent

"O Lord my God!"
In anthem praise,
Ring his final words amid the strife,
'Twas not the cry of desperate fright,
But praise from his victorious life.

A man of God,
Throughout his days,
Whose life stands above the crowd.
His words were full of love and truth,
And his actions spoke out loud.

'Twas not by chance, he came our way,
For such lights are heaven sent.
And though they pass too soon from view,
They mark clear the path by which they went.

"O Lord my God!"
We each wonder, "What shall we do?"
Save in thy grace like him we'll trust,
And like him still follow you.

## At Heaven's Morning Roll Call

When the men in blue made roll call,
At the start of every shift,
They would hear Duncan answer, "Present!"
And it gave every man a lift.

He answered with such assurance,
That courage he would inspire,
In the others serving with him,
Though their lives be under fire.

When the preacher took attendance,
There he sat reverent in his pew.
Duncan was always present,
Seeking Christ to lead him through.

He worshiped with such devotion,
That faith he would inspire,
In the lives of all who knew him,
Then they'd lean on the Lord much higher.

Now at heaven's morning roll call,
That marks God's eternal dawn,
The Major has answered, "Present!"
For Duncan has gone home.

He answers with such victory,
That it rings through heaven's ranks,
And those who loved him here on earth ,
Cannot but with him send their thanks.

Dr. C.R. Hill, Jr.

## Heaven Bound on the Evening Breeze

She has sailed on many a journey far,
Before setting out for the streets of gold,
Yet nothing on those other trips,
Can compare to what she will now behold.

Nor can the suffering she has endured,
Match the glory she now sees,
Nor can we yet here comprehend,
What awaits for them whom Jesus frees.

Too many here live in an illusion false,
Thinking life on earth will never end.
But the truth is that it is very brief –
It appears – then gone like a puff of wind.

Yet she was not like one of those,
Though she traveled far and wide,
For this trip she planned long ago,
When she chose Jesus to be her guide.

Other voyages were on charted seas,
Where vessels of iron could go,
Yet the chart for life's greatest voyage,
One only can through Jesus know.

So her port call now has come,
And she set sail on the evening breeze,
To her inheritance that shall never fade,
Keep for all whom Jesus from sin frees.

## When you Meet in Heaven's Dawn

In just the twinkling of an eye,
More than eighty years have flown,
Now comes the momentary sadness,
To all on earth who him have known.

Yet tears of sorrow are passing things,
For all the joys his life has brought;
His gentle ways of kindness shown,
Have your hearts thanksgiving taught.

A man like him is rarely found,
Among the masses this day and time.
A man who always thankful was,
And to all he met so extra kind.

Four score and more he was with us,
A lengthy life by human measure.
Yet for all who loved him here,
Too short a time for such a treasure.

Now you see through sorrow's tears,
As from your presence he has gone,
But tears of joy shall flood your heart,
When again you meet in heaven's dawn.

Dr. C.R. Hill, Jr.

## Heaven's Porch Light

Sit  Patches!
Stay for a little talk.
We've passed here often ,
While on our evening walk.

That house has been dark before,
Though it's darker now than then.
'Twas then from an hour late,
As her mistress slept within.
"Miss" Frankie's gone.
Moved as planned;
Though not next door,
But to a brighter sweeter land.
How dark those windows are.
Wait, look how above the roof,
Shines bright that evening star!
Is that Venus?
I've seen her thus 'fore dawn,
Or could it be "Miss" Frankie,
Has left Heaven's porch light on?

78

## Taking Leave in Autumn

Autumn seems the time to leave,
The time when life with grace can end.
The soul can shed its robe of flesh,
And soar homeward on the wind.

In early spring a mountain woods,
Is clothed in dogwood flowers fair.
But the finest gowns that woodlands boast,
Must wait until autumn is in the air.

This gracious lady did think it thus,
Though she was much in love with life,
For she had known it all and lived it well,
As a mother, friend, and wife.

Through her spring and summer years,
She was refined with grace and charm.
But her finest beauty was for autumn kept,
Then she rose to heavenly arms.

A dogwood tree against a winter sky,
Appears stark and dead and bare,
But touch its limbs with spring's soft breath,
And again it is clothed in flowers fair.

And as a dear one lies in state,
It appears that all life and love are gone,
But the soul's the tree that in springtime blooms,
And in heaven lives on and on.

## The Music of His Life

Heaven got a laugh that night,
When Harry cleared the gate.
They'd been longing for a Murphy joke,
And they could no longer wait.

"Top of the morning," Peter said,
As Harry strolled in straight and tall,
"And the shank of the day to you," said he,
"It is great to see you-all."

Then laying all his jokes aside,
He approached the heavenly throne,
And reverently thanked the Lord of Life,
For all the grace he'd shown.

Some times humor is just a sham,
To cover up one's fear,
But when it springs from deep within,
It's because one walks with Jesus near.

That was the way of things in Harry's case,
His humor rose from a deeper spring,
For Jesus dwelt within his heart,
Which caused his soul to sing.

It was the music of his life we heard,
In his love for a hearty joke,
And the joy of his walk with Christ,
Spilled out whenever Harry spoke.

## In My Eternal Strength

"According to the days I give,
I will supply you with my strength,
With the rising of each new day's sun,
Until your days have reached full length.

If you will set your course by me,
And make your own the cross I bear;
Then all your days you can call on me,
And you will always find me there.

The strength of soul and sure resolve,
Of character strong and true,
If others you will value high,
I shall bestow on you.

Then as your life has run its course,
When your days have reached full length;
I shall bear you up upon my wings,
As a youth in my eternal strength."

Dr. C.R. Hill, Jr.

# In the House of God's Abode

"I love Thy kingdom, Lord,
The house of Thine abode...",
Could well Sue's motto have been,
For in all of her being it glowed.

Sunshine always attended her way,
With her, Christ's joy was always near.
Whenever she entered a house or room,
She filled the whole place with her cheer.

Her life was full of the songs of faith,
From God's most heavenly Word.
Her love held fast like a solid rock,
For her family, her friends, and her Lord.

So sudden now she's gone from us,
From beyond our touch and our sight.
She has taken leave of the walls of earth,
To be robed in heaven's great light.

In heaven for sure she is singing today,
As in her God she is ever abiding.
And in the mansion that Jesus has built for her,
Be assured Sue is forever residing.

## A Mountain Flower Blooming

A flower bloomed in a mountain vale,
Of a fragrance rare and sweet.
This flower showered her joyous light,
Upon all she chanced to meet.

Unlike so many flowers in bouquets,
That quickly bloom then fade,
Mountain flowers are of hardy stock,
So through the years she's stayed.

And with the passing seasons' suns,
This flower's radiance has grown,
To brighten lives wherever she went,
And of all whom she has known.

Though sunset years are upon her now,
Her beauty yet shows clear.
And though her bloom may one day fade,
Her seeds will yet bloom here.

O' if you should one day pass by here,
And a mountain flower should appear,
Pause and admire how she,
Keeps on blooming year by year.

Dr. C.R. Hill, Jr.

# A Fisherman's Farewell

I think I'd like to fish tomorrow,
Take my boat out on the lake.
I'll be leaving early dear,
And be fishing when you wake.

Don't worry now that I'm not here,
When you in the morning rise,
I will have gone after fishing here,
To receive the Master Fisherman's prize.

For years you know I've labored long,
And always trusted in God's grace,
Now at the end of my fishing days,
I will be looking upon God's face.

I will have sailed the crystal sea,
And walked up the streets of gold.
I am singing now those songs of praise,
With the saints and friends of old.

Parting here is always sad,
It is a time for shedding tears.
But sorrow's tears will turn to joy,
When we are with Jesus for endless years.

## Through Ageless Seasons Singing

With the leaves of autumn nearly gone,
And the sky a winter gray,
Mother chose to avoid the winter chill,
So she left for heaven today.

She watched many autumns come and go,
From her home on Muriel's hill,
There like the leaves that know their time,
She learned to yield to heaven's will.

Thus when the season for her life,
Had reached its final chime,
She rejoiced that the bell had tolled,
Then to heaven she did climb.

With the cross of Jesus as her bridge,
And his faithful hand to hold,
She left the change that seasons bring,
Before another winter's cold.

Now in the warmth of Jesus' love,
At the throne of heavens' king,
She'll with the heavenly host join in,
And through the ageless seasons sing.

Dr. C.R. Hill, Jr.

## With the Christmas Christ Now Gone

The manger scenes she viewed for years,
She'd watched the Christmas Candles burn,
'Twas to see the Christ that Christmas heralds,
That her faithful heart did yearn.

So as the day when we recall his birth,
Grew ever nearer and nearer,
She took her leave from Christmas scenes,
To be with our Christmas Christ so dear.

For the hope so long ago she'd found,
At his manger beneath her tree,
Was when her life on earth was through,
The Christ of Christmas she would see.

Now in his heavenly presence stands,
This one whom Jesus Christ loved so,
And all the wonder of heaven grand,
She did this Christmas know.

And you who bade her last farewells,
This year on Christmas Eve,
Will also some day be with her,
For you the Christmas Christ believe.

## On The Wings of Grace

As eagles soar on outstretched wings,
He lived to mount the sky,
To free himself from earth's restraints,
And on silver wings to fly.

'Twas the dream he lived to fill,
He spent his happiest hours,
Above the clouds where eagles soar,
On wings with lifting powers.

But flying craft are made by men,
So must alas come always down.
And men are creatures made for earth,
To live first upon the ground.

'Tis here upon the wings of love,
That men must strive to fly,
To learn the skills that lift the soul,
Beyond earth's clouds and sky.

While in this flight school yet enrolled,
He has now lifted from this life,
To test the Spirit's wings of grace,
And soar above all earthly strife.

## In Heaven's Finished Room

He's asleep now.
Such a peaceful heavenly rest,
That though it hurts to give him up,
It is clearly for the best.

So long he fought,
Struggling for each breath.
That much in love with life was he,
Though he had no fear of death.

He held Christ's hand,
Who was victor over the tomb.
He knew when life on earth was done,
We would enter heaven's finished room.

With fears long gone,
His faith was fixed on God.
Now his soul will live on high,
As his body rests beneath the sod.

He's asleep now.
Or he appears to be to us.
But in heaven above he is wide awake,
As he greets the Christ he trusts.

## In A House Not Made With Hands

A loving wife, a sister dear,
A treasure to us all,
Has taken leave of us below,
To answer God's heavenward call.

For forty years you walked together,
Along life's wonderful trail,
Now she has gone to receive the house,
God has built for her beyond the veil.

Through years of faith you've built for this,
Yet the heart can't help but weep,
For the price we each must pay for love,
Is sorrow when comes death's sleep.

But sleep it is and nothing more,
For while the soul is at home with God,
The house now resting here below,
Will rise again from beneath the sod.

So go ahead and shed your tears.
Fill the empty place within your heart.
But hold fast the promise God gives of life,
Where we never again shall part.

## I'll Meet You at the River

"I'll meet you at the river,"
Jesus said so long ago,
"I'll walk with you the distance,
And never ever let you go."

With Jesus as her shepherd,
Jane feared not what was ahead,
She held firm her hope of heaven,
For she trusted what he said.

As she drew near the chilly Jordan,
Where from this life she would cross,
She held no fear of dying,
Because in Christ life knows no loss.

Now for you who her must follow,
When your course on earth is through,
She would urge you walk with Jesus,
That at the river he'll meet you too.

Then in heaven you will be united,
Around the throne at Jesus' feet,
Where with saints from all the ages,
God's eternal praise you will repeat.

## Heaven's Glad Tomorrow

On Jordan's stormy banks we stood,
Where Gene tarried for a while,
Then he turned and started home,
To greet God's waiting smile.

Jesus came to walk with him,
Across the river wide;
Then he tarried a moment more,
Just on the other side.

We stood by and watched them leave,
As though walking hand in hand,
Far behind the pains of earth,
Ahead, God's promised land.

Arm in arm they seemed to stroll,
Out beyond the Milky Way,
They went on to greet the dawn,
Of heaven's eternal day.

Though it pains us to let him go,
And our hearts do ache with sorrow,
Yet, we release him in joy and hope,
Looking to heaven's glad tomorrow.

Dr. C.R. Hill, Jr.

## With Happy Memories Dear

In quiet celebration now,
We come to say goodbye,
In joyful affirmation of,
The home she's gained on high..

Here below 'tis through veils of tears,
We give up the ones we love.
But they arrive to shouts of joy,
When they finally reach their home above.

Thus, we gather here this morn,
Still on the Friday side of life,
But she's awakened to Easter praise,
Beyond all earthly pain and strife.

Oh, that we too may one day gain,
Our home within God's land.
The home which Jesus bought for us,
With nail-pierced feet and hands.

Until that day may we remain,
With happy memories dear,
And in the warmth the love she showed,
Always feel that she is near.

## On Morning's Wings

O' give me the wings of the morning,
Let me climb with the rising sun.
I've finished the course set before me,
The race that was mine has been run.

I'll rise to the mansion that awaits me,
The room Jesus went to prepare.
By His grace and His blood He forgave me,
He will greet me when I take to the air.

I cherish the time that I've spent here.
There are loved ones I'll miss as I leave.
But I bid you to look to that morning,
Then miss me, but try not to grieve.

For in heaven we will gather immortal.
God Himself will dry all our tears,
And we will dwell there with Jesus rejoicing,
Unmolested by earth's worries and fears.

Dr. C.R. Hill, Jr.

## Papa's House

Papa's house is empty now,
His dogs know something's wrong.
It is suddenly a very lonely place,
Now that Papa Bill is gone.

His house was always a joyful place,
For a boy and girl to come,
Despite the sorrows known to older hearts,
To be at Papa's house was fun.

But now for him as soon for all,
His time on earth is through,
And he has moved to be with God,
In a heavenly home that's new.

Up there the sorrows that rob life's joy,
And break the hearts of men,
Are washed away; made void of power,
So joy is made new again.

Oh, none of us would gain this prize,
Based on what we here have done.
Such a hope resides in one thing alone,
That is in Jesus Christ, God's Son.

So Papa's house is empty now,
For the homes of earth must pass.
Now Papa has a heavenly home,
Which in Christ will last and last.

## A Light Still Shining

The morning sky was autumn blue,
The rising sun like a diamond bright,
When Bessie Goodman stepped from earth,
Into heaven's glorious light.

O' I should wish to go as she,
To meet the rising sun,
When my life measures full of years,
And my task on earth is done.

For here she lived in quiet faith,
Like a tree by the river grounded,
And brought forth fruits of love and grace,
In the hope her Savior founded.

In heaven Jesus prepares the room,
For all who trust his grace.
On earth to have one's children's praise,
'Tis life's sweetest nectar taste.

Now Bessie Goodman's laid to rest,
Amid our tears of earthly sorrow,
But her life well lived still lights the way,
To the joy of God's tomorrow.

Dr. C.R. Hill, Jr.

# Margaret's Song

I have gone home by the Master's road,
The way Jesus has opened for me.
I will dine tonight at the table of God,
Where with Jesus my savior I'll be.

I shall never complain of the lot I was cast,
For God's goodness to me undeserved;
Has exceeded my tears, my sorrows, or my pain,
And has my  place at God's table reserved.

'Tis not the thing to grieve that I am gone,
Oh, I know my presence you'll miss,
But I have been living - my whole life long,
To inherit my crown, and this bliss.

Life is a journey, we must all travel along;
One just cannot remain in one place!
The high road for home I've traveled in life,
In the hope I'd at last see God's face.

So weep not my dear ones although I am gone,
But come home by the road that I've trod;
And we'll meet again at the foot of the throne,
Where we will sit down to dinner with God.

## Diamonds on the Cheek

We walked with her to the river's edge,
There we watched her as she crossed,
Until beyond the horizon she disappeared,
And to our earthly shore was lost.

Yet though our tear-stained face be sad,
We harbor hope within our heart,
For soon we too will cross that stream,
And there nevermore shall part.

Though we cannot see it now,
Nor even comprehend,
The glory God has waiting there,
We know our lives will never end.

For it is Jesus who has promised it,
To all who upon him do rely,
That though we pass from earthly view,
In him we'll never die.

Yea, from the grave he has risen up,
To prove to us this truth,
That while on earth we may grow old,
In heaven we'll have eternal youth.

So let the diamonds stain your cheeks,
Go ahead and taste their brim.
They speak of love you shared on earth,
And love you'll share beyond all time.

## To God's Eternal Day

We spoke of love that never ends,
When Charlotte crossed the bar,
Today Gray too has taken leave,
And together now they are.

Blessed we've been these extra years,
To have him with us remain,
But he has longed to go home to her,
And like her to heaven gain.

Complete they are now in heaven's home,
To roam this earth no more,
Yet for us in the lives they lived,
They have left us a map to heaven's door.

So take your comfort in God's promise sweet,
That beyond the bounds of earth and time,
There awaits for those who have faith in him,
A home built by the Master's own design.

May we each mark well the road they chose,
And walk faithful in his way,
Until we like they have crossed the bar,
To God's eternal Day.

## From All His Labors Rested

In the mist that veils the sleeping bay,
A ship at anchor rested.
Then came the call to sail that day,
His life being fully tested.

'Twas no storm with wind awhirl,
To tear him from his mooring,
But with anchor weighed his sails unfurl,
And his bow was seaward soaring.

True he lingered long with us,
As in the harbor he made ready,
To launch his voyage in trust,
On a course mapped sure and steady.

Seems some ships sail with the morning tide,
While others on a storm's mad swelling,
'Tis for what they stood and the good they tried,
That long after will still be telling

From the mist that veils the sleeping bay,
A good ship sound and  tested,
Set out upon this homeward way,
And from all his labors rested.

Dr. C.R. Hill, Jr.

## Fishing with God's Son

He'd gone fishing with his son,
They caught their limit, too.
Then he took his final homeward turn,
As his fishing here was through.

It was not for him a sad goodbye,
He'd known the time was near.
So he lived each day while waiting,
Holding every moment dear.

Yet he looked for God's tomorrow,
With ever increasing hope,
Knowing when he crossed the river,
He'd live on a grander scope.

It was a promise he received,
One he heard his Savior Jesus tell,
That when life on earth was finished,
He would in heaven with Jesus dwell.

So now in heaven's sunshine,
With his earthly race now run,
We can see him today in heaven,
Going fishing with God's Son.

## To Heaven's Shore

No lingering on I wish to do,
No staying beyond my time.
I'll live each day to the full degree,
And when evening comes I'll recline.

I'll take my leave with the waning moon,
By the star that precedes the sun.
For with the morning's awakening chorus,
My work on earth shall be done.

I'll be swiped away to heaven's shore,
There a mansion stands ready and new,
Awaiting my final woman's touch,
And there I'll be waiting for you.

So weep not long as I take my leave,
For the love we have shared is not done.
It has merely moved to God's glorious realm,
Where it will grow in the light of His Son.

Dr. C.R. Hill, Jr.

## Someday Will Be Homecoming

Some days I had a good day,
I woke up feeling fine.
Throughout the day I'd sit and visit,
As dropped in old friends of mine.

Some days I had to struggle,
Just to see the hours through.
I'd sit quietly reminiscing,
There was nothing more to do.

Some days I'd dream about her,
My loving, life-long mate.
She set sail this time of year,
Of being with her I'd dream and wait.

Some days I'd see the old house,
Where we lived our married years.
Some days I'd see a new house,
Where God dries earth's lonely, sad tears.

Some days I'd sit contented,
Thanking God for years of grace.
Some days I'd dream of heaven,
Where he has prepared for us a place.

Some days were long and boring,
With the same old T.V. drumming.
But I'd sit there patiently, knowing,
That someday would be Homecoming.

## In Gardens of Glory

Supper finished and her plant repaired,
From the storm that had passed our way,
She bid all good night and closed her eyes,
Then greeted life's close of day.

For as she slept in tranquil rest,
Through the calm 'twixt dust and dawn,
The angels came and gently called,
Then took Flo to her heavenly home.

It always hurts when a loved one dear,
Sets sail at life's close of day.
But it is a comfort, too, when no storm precedes,
As they just peacefully sail away.

And there is no surprise or doubt of mind,
As to where her voyage has ended.
She has sailed from here to the Father's house,
With Jesus whom she has long befriended.

For certain we are at that mansion above,
In that land of days ne'er ending,
There is a garden in bloom with plants galore,
Just waiting for Flo to be tending.

Dr. C.R. Hill, Jr.

## A Champion Now At Home

Our champion bowled his final game,
Then he laid his trophies down.
He exchanged the glory they stood for,
For a far more glorious crown.

The games in life he'd lost and won,
Were but events in time,
But 'twas to the victory Jesus won,
He had all his life resigned.

O he resisted long the challenge,
To yield himself to Jesus' name,
But when at last he did concede,
He bowled entirely in God's lanes.

Joy danced in his twinkling eyes,
Like no strike of pins could bring.
His grip of honest heartfelt love,
Said he'd found Jesus as his King.

His grip so strong for gentle hands,
Showed him a man of Godly grace,
Touched by the hands that on the cross,
Had been pierced in his place.

O now from all his earthly games,
And his songs of joy and praise,
He has come at last to the Father's house,
Where he sings on for ceaseless days.

## The Fording of Heaven's Stream

Another Saint has crossed the bar,
On an afternoon in May,
With the warmth of spring upon his face,
He crossed at the closing of the day.

His years were long with us below,
His gentle ways so full of grace,
Straight and tall he stood in stature,
Kindness wore well upon his face.

Faith was the hallmark of his soul,
His love for Jesus to all well known,
In the pathway of God's knowledge,
Through the years he true had grown.

His place among us will be missed,
Yet our sorrow shall not long last,
For his life had achieved its purpose,
It was for heaven his lot was cast.

The river's edge he gained at evening,
There with Jesus he made the ford,
Then arm in arm on up the pathway,
To his home built by the Lord.

Dr. C.R. Hill, Jr.

# In Tribute to a Steel Magnolia

Steel Magnolias, southern flowers,
That grow not upon our trees,
But are grown in quiet grace,
Through time spent on their knees,

The wives of giants they tend to be,
Who by them are giants made,
Men who grow to their full height,
In the shadows of their standards' shade,

Frail and delicate they appear,
Yet in strength that resembles steel,
In resilience bouncing back,
Never minding what life may deal.

Yet even these like flowers all,
Reach their time to fade,
But not before others bloom,
In the difference they have made.

So comes again that time in life,
When from us such a flower is taken,
And added to the bouquet of heaven,
Where in new beauty she will awaken.

# A Runner's Early Finish

A son has gone from beyond our reach,
We can no longer him embrace;
Nor can we again hold his hand,
Or look here upon his face.

It is our hope that through Jesus Christ,
He on leaving did heaven gain,
And though he no longer dwells with us,
He in our hearts will yet remain.

Too soon life's race for him was run,
Too quickly came the finish line.
His course was short over rocky ground,
Then he reached the shores of time.

Now we who linger yet on earth,
By him do value more each day,
And check to see if the path we run,
Does match the Christ made way.

O' may it be by God's great grace,
That our paths again with his will cross,
And by God's mercy not his soul or ours,
Will Jesus allow to forever be a loss.

Dr. C.R. Hill, Jr.

# In God's Never Ending Day

Mother slipped away this week,
With Monday morning's dawn,
Her long journey now complete,
Her life's victory finally won.

The hollow place she leaves behind,
In the hearts who knew her love,
Must now give way to being filled,
By knowing she is with God above.

And by taking hold of the legacy,
That she to each of you bequeaths,
The faith that earth is just the start,
For one who in Jesus Christ believes.

O' take this time to shed your tears,
Then dry your eyes again,
Your mother exchanged this life of clay,
For that life which will never end.

And the great desire she has for you,
Is that you walk the Christ-lead way,
That once again you will be with her,
In God's never ending day.

## On the Wings of Evening's Wind

How long the night did around her draw,
As earth's sights and sounds did fade.
Yet for her love of life itself,
She long with us had stayed.

Her quiet manner and gentle grace,
Received each day as precious gift,
And without use of words her being yet,
Did those around her spirit's lift.

Still whether the night be long or short,
Darkness soon gives way to dawn,
And the souls who tarried here awhile,
Arise and to heaven move along.

So it was as evening shadows grew,
As the night watch began again,
She bid farewell to the earth she loved,
And took the wings of evening's wind.

In heaven now her long night is done,
Heaven's light does her heart inspire,
On her ears falls the joyful carols,
Of heaven's welcoming morning choir.

Dr. C.R. Hill, Jr.

## Sailing From the Shores of Time

Today, Virginia put out to sea,
On that voyage that awaits us all.
From the shores of time to eternity,
She received her Father's call.

She labored long upon our fair shore,
A life of service rendered with love.
Now on the wings of the morning breeze,
She has set sail for service above.

She'll be missed in our familiar port,
By the many friends she held so dear.
But she arrived at home to songs of joy,
When on heaven's shore she did appear.

Now as the wake of any parting ship,
Leaves a churning, foaming brine,
May our tears prepare our hearts,
For the voyage we'll make from time.

## Christmas Day in the Evening

'Twas Christmas day in the evening,
When William from time set forth,
On that journey with his Master,
Far beyond the fields of earth.

For years he tilled the soil,
Of earth's good fertile fields,
He'd sow his seeds in season,
And in season reap their yields.

God must take a special liking,
To the men who work the land,
Who risk all they have to grow things,
And must trust God's gracious hand.

Yes, it must have been from farming,
William learned that over all,
If you'll trust God in the spring time,
He won't forget you in the fall.

Thus, William came unto his autumn,
Holding fast his Master's hand,
And on Christmas day in the evening,
He went with Jesus to work His land.

# The Anchors of God's Grace

Like a raging hurricane,
The storm of death has come,
To take your loved one from your midst,
His course of life now run.

Now the rocks along life's shore,
Threaten your life also to undo,
With doubt, despair and disbelief,
How will you ever make it through?

Here are some anchors for your soul,
That will help you to endure life's storm.
Hold fast to them in this dark night,
And pray for God's new day to dawn.

For God is with you in these waves,
His provision holds you secure.
His pardon rebukes the winds of sin,
As forever will his love endure.

Now your loved one's ship has landed,
Far beyond earth's ferocious storms,
Safely at his home port moored,
Secure forever in his Savior's arms.

## With Eagle's Wings She Flies

Some walk the upward trail of earth,
With strength to the very end,
While others rest along the way,
Their strength gone from every limb.

It matters not at the end of day,
If they walked on until day was through,
Or sat a spell beside the trail,
To reflect upon the view.

In the end when day is done,
And the crossing has been made,
Each joins the happy band of those,
Whose debt on Golgotha Jesus paid.

'Tis then that all with equal strength,
Will with eagle's wings mount up,
Then sit at the table spread for them,
Where they will with Jesus share the cup.

Then in the light from God's own throne,
As eternal ages pass on by,
They will dwell with Jesus there,
In their heavenly dwelling built on high.

Dr. C.R. Hill, Jr.

## Rejoicing on the Dance Floor

A Southern gentleman, full of grace,
To heaven has taken leave.
In his place there is a mighty void,
As all we who loved him grieve.

Yet our grieving is not for him,
For it is to his destiny he has gone,
It is for ourselves who remain behind,
Because his life gave us a song.

When I would play golf with him,
And he'd be on the green in three,
"I'll see you on the dance floor."
Were the words he'd say to me.

He in heaven now rejoices,
As friends and loved ones him embrace.
He has received the reward he sought,
As he beholds his Savior's face.

The years he spent on earth with us,
Seem a very lengthy span,
Yet they were not even a single tick,
Of heaven's second hand.

Still we found them long enough,
To mark the path on which he trod,
As through the maze of earthly trials,
He took Jesus' path that led to God.

## The Sailing of a Saint

Another saint set sail today,
Across life's crystal sea,
From the painful shores of time,
His soul now gains eternity.

The shell he used to travel here,
Had grown weak and worn with time;
While his spirit all the stronger grew,
Through his Savior's grace divine.

He had been a leader here with us,
One who was a doer of God's Word,
Through his daily habits and faithful acts,
The love of Christ was clearly heard.

Now large footprints he leaves behind,
For each one of us to trace,
Until we too shall sail across that sea,
And behold there our Savior's face.

We'll pause a moment to shed our tears,
For our hearts shall miss him here.
Yet we rejoice through our trust in Christ,
Knowing we will with him in heaven appear.

Dr. C.R. Hill, Jr.

## Today in Heaven I Wear a Smile

The rubble that before you lies,
Is not the place I am.
Today I dwell in a palace grand,
Built by the Master Builder's hand.

In Jesus with whom I've always walked,
I set out to others serve,
When came the quake that took my life,
In the rubble you there observe.

It matters not my length of life,
Or what seems my unfair death.
But rather that throughout each day,
It was from Jesus I drew my breath.

So when I went in service there,
It was not to live or die.
It was that by serving others I'd serve,
Him who built my mansion here on high.

No greater love he once had said,
Has anyone than this,
Than to give themselves for another's sake,
That one shall not God's favor miss.

So grieve a moment; I know you must,
For we have been parted for a while.
But as you think of me with tearful eyes,
Know today in heaven I wear a smile.

## God's Home of Endless Day

Daddy left for home today,
From his house on Toonigh Road.
He labored hard these latter days,
Beneath life's ever increasing load.

He has finished now the upward climb,
On this section of life's trail,
And he waits for you around the bend,
Across the stream beyond the veil.

Although the path seems long to you,
The distance really is not great,
We will all be crossing one by one,
To where our gathered loved ones wait.

So dry the tears that stain your faces,
Look up instead and smile.
Across the stream beyond the veil,
We will be reunited after while.

But until we reach that place,
Where ends this section of our way,
We must continue the upward climb,
Towards God's home of endless day.

Dr. C.R. Hill, Jr.

## His Love Runs with You Still

The steady course of life is run,
His race is finished now.
No more the strain of upward climb,
Gone the sweat upon his brow.

He ran his race with faithful strides,
Nor did he the hills resent.
For throughout the course he always knew,
His strength was heaven-sent.

In Christ his Lord, he did always trust,
He sought to serve him well,
And in the final stretch of life,
One could sure that friendship tell.

Today he's crossed the finish line.
He does now in heaven run.
His legs renewed with heaven's strength,
On his brow the crown he's won.

So run your race, yet incomplete,
Yea, run with greater will,
For though no longer at your side,
His love runs with you still.

## Among the Hills of Time

His campaign now is ended,
The final taps is blown.
New orders have been issued.
The Colonel has transferred home.

He is laid to rest beneath the sacred sod,
Where his love in live had bloomed.
By the river where he met his wife,
Where he became her dashing groom.

His campaign continued long from there,
Down the winding course of years,
Through times as bright as autumn woods,
And dark as winter vales of tears.

He was a man of complex weave,
With an upward marching stride,
Sometimes as soft as an autumn breeze,
Sometimes an ocean's storm-tossed tide.

Now the final taps has sounded,
To the guns in proud reply,
His flag is neatly folded,
Never more to grace the sky.

Still all is not yet finished,
For he now lives with the Hills sublime,
While his spirit marches onward,
Among the Hills of time.

Dr. C.R. Hill, Jr.

## The Resetting of the Sails

It was during Sunday's sacred hour,
That he steeped from earth and time.
How often he has cheated death,
Only finally to resign.

Yet 'tis not how many lives one has,
Or the length of years one lives.
It is the character of the heart and soul,
That to a life the meaning gives.

His was of the richest kind,
In spirit like God's Son,
He did not fit the standard mold,
But was a noble race he'd run.

Life to him was often cruel,
Yet it was kindness he did return,
To those who dealt him hurtful blows,
He dealt forgiveness they could not earn.

When the storms against him hurled,
Some cold and bitter gale,
He'd set the sail within his soul,
And to another victory sail.

Ah when at Sunday's sacred hour,
He did appear to at last succumb,
He'd merely set the sails anew,
And sailed home, his victory won.

## She Walks in Heaven's Light

Through the years she faithfully walked,
Holding Jesus' hand and mine;
Until we reached the water's edge,
Where she stepped beyond the shores of time.

Oh the love she drew from God,
Then passed along to me,
As together we served his flocks,
On this side of heaven's sea.

Her beauty I did daily view,
Radiant with God's grace;
While in her quiet steady ways,
I discerned the image of God's face.

The faith we shared these many years,
Has been our anchor through life's storms.
And though in faith I give her up,
I yet long to hold her in my arms.

I yearn once more to see her face,
And to have her by my side;
So I will keep this path we've trod,
Until I too, step over Jordan's tide.

While in the wake of the life she lived,
I will yet other souls invite,
To place their hand in Jesus' palm,
Then walk by faith in heaven's light.

Dr. C.R. Hill, Jr.

## At the Water's Edge

Once again at the water's edge,
I hold a loved one's hand,
As we gaze across Old Jordan's brim,
To Canaan's promised land.

O will she cross the chilly flow,
To the safety of that shore?
Or will the current sweep her away,
To be heard from never more?

The question haunts the honest heart,
That begs to really know,
When we release our hands on earth,
Where will my dear one go?

That current surely swift and cold,
Would sweep every soul away,
Had grace not made a ford for us,
To God's eternal day.

So unto him who calms the storm,
And still walks the churning sea,
I'll look to bear her safely o'er,
While his Spirit comforts me.

Then as we let our hands release,
And exchange our final wave,
I'll lean upon that living hope,
Jesus bought beyond the grave.

## Sailing with the Evening Tide

I've taken sail with the evening tide,
Over the waning moonlit sea.
I am crossing over to the other side,
Where Jesus awaits to welcome me.

I know my leaving will cause you pain,
But your sorrow is for season brief.
You will find joy in hope for I'll see you again,
While from my suffering I've been granted relief.

I've journeyed on to my heavenly home,
Where my inheritance has forever been.
Now by God's grace and love you will carry on,
Until in his presence we'll be together again.

Hold fast the faith that we cherished below,
That served as compass and guide and chart,
And remember the love that gave us life,
Then hold steady God's course in your heart.

The days of earth are fleeting at best,
They are given for faith to mature,
Those who through their trials shall stand the test,
Will taste of life in Jesus secure.

Dr. C.R. Hill, Jr.

## A Saint with No Fear

I met a saint the other day,
Who was nearing the end of life's trail,
Yet I saw no fear in her face at all,
As she prepared to enter the veil.

Indeed I saw there on her face,
A look of contentment and peace,
As from her sufferings here down below,
She looked forward to receiving release.

She was looking beyond to an eternal place,
God has built for her without hands.
His Spirit within her was his guarantee,
That his promise in Jesus firmly stands.

O you her loved ones will weep for a while,
For tears are the price paid for love.
But don't be disheartened or think it the end,
You will be with her again up above.

So keep to the path that she followed in life,
The way made for us all by our Lord,
Hold on to the hand of God's only Son,
And live every day by God's Word.

# He Played the Game for God

Today the Coach received the call,
He was taken from our game,
And playing on without him here,
Will seem not to us the same.

A teacher he who sought the best,
From every member of his squad,
He taught us on the gridiron field,
To play the game for God.

"Your natural skills are gifts to you,
The field of life will be your test,
And only you choose in the game,
To give to God your very best."

Words like these far more than said,
To each player that he coached,
He lived them out in faithful ways,
With every play that he approached.

Now summoned from his final play,
As we recall the gridiron sod,
With Jesus coaching at his side,
He taught us to play the game for God.

Dr. C.R. Hill, Jr.

## The Home with Heaven's View

Mommy Hull awoke in heaven today.
Earth's long sleep now through.
In a mansion built especially for her,
Just as Jesus said He would do.

She lingered long down here below,
With those in life she'd loved,
While through the night of earth's long sleep,
Her spirit watched the work above.

Her country home was once the place,
For happy, joy-filled days,
Where with her husband at her side,
They did their family raise.

Then when his time and life was o'er,
The country house put on a frown.
So she sold, and packed it up,
And built her house in town.

It, too, a home with joy and mirth,
Where grandchildren came to sleep.
But when they grew more on their own,
A house was too much to keep.

She moved again, and then twice more,
Each time she required less space,
Until now she's moved to her heavenly home,
With the view looking on God's face.

## On the Passing of a Friend

A friend of mine went home today.
Her life's journey too soon ended.
But she is there with the Father now,
And Jesus whom she had befriended.

Our paths had long together run,
Through many sun filled years,
And I know she had a dwelling place,
Beyond life's veil of tears.

Though her leaving makes us sad below,
And we would long to hear her voice.
There is comfort in the knowledge we have,
That she doth now in heaven rejoice.

A friend of mine went home today,
Another one in line,
Has climbed life's steep and winding road,
And gained heaven's heights sublime.

Dr. C.R. Hill, Jr.

## The Homeward Leading Lane

He took the homeward leading lane,
While still lingered summer's day,
Then slowly walked 'neath autumn's sun,
As we shared with him the homeward way.

We sat together in quiet thought,
As we did his life and love recall,
And thus we shared the homeward lane,
As autumn leaves from the trees did fall.

Then as the days took on a morning chill,
Neath autumn skies so clear and bright,
We reached the gate in the homeward lane,
Where he bid each of us good night.

He then walked on beyond our view,
To climb heaven's front porch step,
As we lingered by the homeward gate,
And held each other as we wept.

Yet in our tears there is no despair,
For Jesus was his homeward way and gate.
So when we take the homeward lane we know,
He will for us on heaven's front porch wait.

## The Lady Has Gone Home

With grace and kindly-gentle ways,
She lived among us here.
Her patient touch and loving smile,
Could turn back the saddest tear.

Good she was to all she met,
Even when good was not deserved,
As for vengeance that she knew,
Was for God alone reserved.

Forgiveness!
That was more her style.
For when forgiven injuries hurt,
But for a little while.

Faithfully she at peace did live,
As through life she'd each day stroll,
And in God's Spirit her daily walk,
Was one of graceful self-control.

Yet there comes a time in every life,
When the heart takes a turn for home,
As feet grown weary of earthly paths,
No longer wish to roam.

And so she too as Norman did,
Into the homeward lane has turned,
For to see him there at Jesus' side,
Is what for these years she has yearned.

Dr. C.R. Hill, Jr.

## Tomorrow's Heavenly Morning Dew

Another trail I see ahead,
That leads from this she's taken.
A golden bridge across a silver stream,
She has built with a faith unshaken.

Now across that bridge and up the trail,
I see her footsteps leading,
As she follows on in eternal light,
From God's Word that she'd been reading.

She'll pause perhaps at the gates of pearl,
And wait for you to come along,
Or perhaps she will go on in,
Drawn in by Angels all in song.

It really is of little concern,
For heaven has no sense of time,
And soon you too will be there with her,
In your new house of God's design.

So shed the tears you must today,
Because she is no longer now with you,
But be assured today's tears of sorrow,
Are tomorrow's heavenly morning dew.

## Her Mansion on Heaven's Side

The room she had was a homey one,
With family pictures all around.
The care she got was filled with love,
But she missed her home in town.

Her window looked upon a yard,
That was likewise kept with care,
Those she loved would often come,
So they could visit with her there.

Yet for all there was of the very best,
That for anyone could be done,
There was the aching of her heart,
That accompanies life's setting sun.

It was the groan that fills the heart,
When it has tasted all this life gives,
And longs to reach that heavenly room,
Where the soul with God forever lives.

So now has come her time in life,
To cross over life's great divide.
There the saints have welcomed her,
To her mansion on heaven's side.

## The Homecoming

Homecoming – autumn days in Athens town,
With Georgia's team between the hedge.
The stands of fans clad in red and black,
Gave these "Dawgs" the winning edge.

Homecoming – good old fashion preaching,
And Sunday dinner on the ground,
An afternoon of Gospel singing,
And God's Holy Spirit coming down.

Homecoming – coming home to Canton,
To spend some time with Mom and Dad,
Gathered around their table,
Recalling good times that we've had.

Homecoming – sometime it's in the present,
Sometimes it looks back upon the past,
Ah, but now it seeks the future,
For Dad has gone home at last.

He has seen his share of football,
He'd been in the cheering stands,
But today he crossed the goal to glory,
Before heaven's cheering fans.

## Come Home Now Child

"Come home now child."
It was an oh so familiar sound,
That so often came at the close of day,
As the evening sun was going down.

"Come home now child."
Her boys had often heard her call,
From the kitchen door,
Since they each were very small.

"Come home now child."
Those words echo through our years,
Telling us the time does come,
For us to leave earth's joys and its tears.

So it was on that morning in July,
From her Father's house above,
Came again that familiar call,
"Come home child to my arms of love."

Then to God's arms she quickly flew,
And up the golden path they strolled,
To the home Jesus built for her,
Where she never shall grow old.

Dr. C.R. Hill, Jr.

# In the Echo of Heart's Love

Who says my mother is now with God,
In heaven's mansion grand?
What proof of this is there for me,
Where my doubting heart can stand?

My broken heart is full of grief!
My soul with guilt cries out!
Does heaven have any word at all,
That can free my mind from doubt?

I long to know that gentle peace,
That tells me all is well,
And lets me know the one so dear,
Does in God's house safely dwell!

"I know my child your deepest hurt,
'Tis but the echo of your love,
But trust in me and take my word,
Your mother is safe above.

"For in the house my love prepared,
And my death on Calvary bought,
She by my resurrection power,
Has found the healing that she sought."

## The Well Blessed Man

Three score and ten, and perhaps ten more,
'Tis life's allotted span.
And he who lives this length of days,
'Tis indeed a well blessed man.

'Twas Johnny's lot to be thus blessed,
With length of life and love;
Thus having run the course of life,
He's crossed the finish line above.

'Twas quiet grace and gratitude,
That I most in him had found.
His love was real and closely held,
For family, church, and town.

O' all who loved him here below,
Are saddened that he's gone,
But gladdened, too, because we know,
That in Jesus he lives on.

Today would mark his day of birth,
He would turn his eightieth page,
Now there is a party in the Father's house,
For his first of endless age.

Dr. C.R. Hill, Jr.

## An Airman's Final Flight

Flying was nothing new to him,
Those Red Tail Airmen he did train,
Then when that war had ended,
He helped us the moon to gain.

Always reaching for greater heights,
For the moon and stars beyond,
He now has reached the highest yet,
As he gained heaven's eternal dawn.

It was not with engines whirling props,
Nor with mighty rockets blast,
But by the grace of God in Christ,
That he has the heavens gained at last.

O you will miss him in the stands,
As Bear and Tiger both compete,
Yet now he cheers from a bleacher higher,
As you strive your journeys to complete.

So until then hold fast the faith,
Walk with Jesus through earth's strife,
And when your time on earth is done,
You'll fly like him to endless life.

## Living on Life's Second Page

A soul steeped out of the shadows today,
From the obscurity imposed by old age,
She once well known, but time marches on,
Now others have walked onto the stage.

Nevertheless, she was still in the wings,
Where she watched from just out of view;
For she still had an appearance to make,
And she was waiting on God for her cue.

Though many today knew not her name,
Because they arrived too late for her part;
Yet her Father above had missed not a line,
For he carried her close to his heart.

Now from her scene, to heaven's applauds,
She has quietly stepped from earth's stage,
And with Jesus beside her she exits this room,
To start living on life's second page.

## This Hero

Heroes come in many forms,
Among the sons of men,
Quiet ones who fought in wars,
They helped our nation win.

They also fight the wars of time,
As families they help raise.
They fill a pew for Sunday Church,
And lift to God their praise.

They move out in the market place,
With honest work each day,
They kneel beside a small child's bed,
And teach them how to pray.

Heroes walk in faithfulness,
Beside the wife they took in youth,
And when life puts them to the test,
They always stand for truth.

A hero may look just like the guy,
You can pass on any street,
But when we gather at God's throne,
Again this hero we will meet.

## God's Tomorrow

A Child was traveling on his way,
When he came upon a trackless wood,
He had no desire for becoming lost,
Yet he must go on as best he could.

The trees o'er head were tall and thick,
The forest dark and dense,
And in the labyrinth of paths,
Of direction he lost all sense.

Feeling all alone and lost,
For home he did despair.
Yet 'tis one who patrols these woods,
Searching out the souls lost there.

When he finds a child there lost,
With a bruised and aching soul,
He takes him in his arms of love,
To his house and makes him whole.

O' that none should stumble upon,
This trackless forest drear,
But truth be told there comes to all,
Some trackless wood of fear.

Yet even in these darkest glens,
Jesus is there to heal our sorrow,
With his promise of redeeming love,
That will make us whole in God's tomorrow.

Dr. C.R. Hill, Jr.

## Fishing With Big Bob

On silver waters I fished with him,
Some ponds and streams alike,
And we spoke of times we'd fish again,
In some stream to which we'd hike.

When our paths would chance to cross,
We'd remember fishing yesterdays.
Then promise that we fish again,
Yet seemed life took us separate ways.

Until I caught the upper view,
Of our silver-watered fishing hole,
Where just around the bend from me,
Was "Big Bob" with his pole.

For almost a half a century now,
Side by side we've fishing been,
In the silver waters of this world,
For souls to Christ to win.

Now with tackle box and rod and reel,
"Big Bob" has left this pond for home,
Where awaits the string of souls,
Who through him have Jesus known.

# A Familiar Home and Crown

There comes a time along life's way,
When things familiar change;
When those we knew no longer are,
And old haunts to us are strange.

Old time itself then plays the thief,
Stealing all our youth away,
Until what hair is left upon our head,
Has faded to shades of gray.

Then it is that our vision shifts,
From the things we once could do,
To the promises God has given us,
Of a life that is forever new.

There is no sadness in moving on,
When our life on earth is spent,
Indeed there's joy in setting out,
To receive the prize that heaven sent.

For if along life's journey's way,
We've kept the path that Jesus laid down,
We'll trade earthly things grown strange,
For a familiar heavenly home and crown.

Dr. C.R. Hill, Jr.

# In God's Homecoming Court

A royal priesthood is what we are,
A race of kings and queens,
That is what the Lord intends,
For all he by his grace redeems.

And so another royal queen,
Has at God's homecoming court arrived,
Death cannot the spirit claim,
Of a queen whom God has made alive.

O' we gather here today,
As do loved ones far away,
Who celebrate the glorious news,
Of their queen's homecoming day.

Here we take the time to pause,
And reflect upon her earthly reign.
How by demonstrating love and faith,
She did the courts of heaven gain.

Her humble manner; her purer heart,
By Jesus made to shine,
She demonstrated in her daily life,
The fruits of grace divine.

To each of you she now bequeaths,
The gift of God's great love,
The way God makes through Jesus Christ,
To become kings and queens above.

## On A Bright November Day

'Twas a bright and sunny November day,
When the leaves were at their best,
And the autumn sky its clearest blue,
That our sister went to rest.

She struggled hard as we stood by,
Through her final moonlit night,
Knowing that the time was near,
When her soul would take its flight.

We held her hand and stroked her brow,
As with her we walked life's ending path,
And though our hearts are sad from loss,
Still we can by God's great promise laugh.

For our God is good and his mercy great,
And does with grace in Christ abound,
So when the lost child looks to him,
He does with love their soul surround.

Yes with her race on earth now run,
And her sufferings all complete,
She walks today on streets of gold,
To bow in thanks at Jesus' feet.

Dr. C.R. Hill, Jr.

# A Man Like His Mountains of Home

From Tennessee he hailed to here.
From mountain stock his frame.
Like those mountains tall he stood,
Hugh Lewis was his name.

A hearty man of commanding ways,
Who lived with vigor and zest.
Whatever task or challenge he faced,
He always strove to be the best.

He loved to laugh and his stories tell,
Of adventures he once knew,
A man of courage who was never afraid,
To tackle an adventure new.

A family man who loved his own,
And provided for them well.
A man whose word was sufficient bond,
Who never his name would sell.

"The world is a bigger place," he'd say,
"Than this tiny town right here."
He'd stood upon some mountain tops,
On some days when the sky was clear.

From Tennessee he had hailed, I said,
A man like his mountains of home.
And a vessel of clay, too restricting a thing,
For a soul who would the heavens roam.

144

## The Impressions of a Saint

In that quiet evening calm,
That whispers day is done,
A saint went home to be with God,
Assured her victory won.

On earth she learned the way of life,
She found what counted most,
And with faith unshaken traced the way,
To reflect her heavenly host.

Hers the kind of heart that knew,
That only love will last,
And the souls of those with love invested,
Would remain when earth is past.

She lingered but a little while,
This saint in love with life,
Then took her leave to be with God,
Above all earthly strife.

Dr. C.R. Hill, Jr.

# The Biggest Race of All

A quiet man finished first that day,
In the biggest race of all.
The race that every mortal must run,
In responding to God's call.

The race is not for earthly fame,
Or the prizes that men give,
'Tis rather run for others' sake,
And gives all that they might live.

That was the race this quiet man,
Had been running all his life.
He spent himself to run it well,
For his children, job, and wife.

Those who win life's biggest race,
May early cross the finish line.
The measure of the race they've run,
Is lives they've touched–not time.

## Where Saints Immortal Stand

Forrest Lovell has crossed the bar,
His victory through trials he won,
By holding firm the hand of God,
And trusting God's great Son.

Years of trial were not wasted here,
Through pain he learned to grow.
As gold refined through melting fire,
So the soul through sufferings glow.

Fires consumed his dross of flesh,
But his gold the brighter grew,
Nor did he forget the way to laugh,
And hold to loved ones true.

In my mind I can see him clear,
On heaven's distant shore,
Standing straight and walking tall,
Where he'll suffer pain no more.

And, I see Jesus reaching out,
His opened, welcoming hand,
To greet him in the victor's ring,
Where saints immortal stand.

Dr. C.R. Hill, Jr.

## As the Saints in Order Go

The saints of time go marching home,
In order one by one.
They graced our lives for many a year,
Now they've joined heaven's Son.

Thus it is Nell has taken leave,
For her mansion in heaven above,
For while on earth she became its heir,
By the purchase of Christ's love.

Though we who linger still in time,
Are saddened because she's gone,
We yet do glean the joy of faith,
That was hers her whole life long.

And in the wake of her leaving us,
Let us assess our lives anew,
So when the final trumpet sounds,
We may join the singing too.

O' on that glad and glorious day,
When we all stand on heaven's shore,
We'll sing our praise to Christ our king,
Where death and sin shall be no more.

## The Echo of His Soul

"You're so good!"
Is what he'd always say.
His words spring from the gratitude,
That was the bedrock of his way.

They were the assessment,
By which he measured men.
I believe they were the reflection,
Of the man he was within.

His mind was like a razor,
His spirit true and kind.
His character was like silver,
Purer and refined.

He rose up the corporate ladder,
While to right remaining true,
And with his quiet manner,
He influenced thousands too.

So when the villain stole him,
Too long before his time,
We stood by in silent sadness,
As the villain stole his mind

Yet the villain had no power,
To take away his soul,
That to Jesus he had given,
And of that Jesus had control.

Whenever I'd go to see him,
He'd keep saying those words again,
And I could hear in them the echo,
Of the friend still living deep within.

## A Dream for Children's Sake

He rested here among these trees,
And the flowers that he raised;
Mowing fields, and mending barns,
Or in a hundred different ways.

He seemed to me a gardener,
Who loved to watch things grow,
And a willing helpful neighbor,
But there was more to him I know.

Behind his restful haven,
With its pastures and its lake,
There was a dream far nobler,
It was all for children's sake.

For he once had a vision,
If a child were steered from wrong,
They would grow up in the way of good,
And live right their whole life long.

So the horses were here for riding,
And the lake for kids to fish.
Here children were taught values,
To give them a chance his only wish.

Now I see him staring out the window,
Looking out on trees and lake,
And I wonder if he is watching,
The lives of children he helped shape.

## The Sendoff of a Friend

Go rest our friend in Jesus' arms,
And the mansion he built for you.
The long and weary road of earth,
Has ended now for you.

Go lend your voice to heaven's choir,
To sing praises to your king,
O let heaven's music fill your heart,
And eternal joy to you bring.

Your way below was fraught with trials,
Many days were filled with pain,
But now you know they cannot compare,
To heaven's wondrous gain.

The tears you shed for loved ones here,
Are now transformed to heaven's jewels,
The pains of earth- life's heavy loads,
Were but heaven's shaping tools,

Now in the glory of eternal day,
Go walk with Christ our friend,
O let the songs you sang on earth,
Be forever sung for Him.

Dr. C.R. Hill, Jr.

## Salute to a Christian Gentleman

A Christian gentleman, that describes him best.
A man of faith longstanding.
Who in his faithful churchmanship,
Was among his peers outstanding.

A Christian gentleman indeed was he,
And of the old school's making.
Why of tie and coat he was never without,
It mattered not how the sun was baking.

But dress and quiet gentle ways,
Are only the surface traits,
Of one who knows he belongs to God,
And who on God's spirit waits.

A Christian gentleman who throughout his days,
Lived by God's great book,
And from its living pages true,
God's daily blessings took.

His quiet manner and faithful ways,
Are the things that we should heed.
For often one speaks loudest when,
He says it with a deed.

## In God's Distant Promise Land

We choose in life the path we walk,
But not what turns that path may take,
It is our response to the turns we're given,
That ready the soul for heaven make.

It mattered not what her path presented,
Either steep climbs or deep descents,
She faithfully walked it with her guide,
Who for her from heaven had been sent.

In trust and quiet fellowship she walked,
Through the scriptures and the hymns.
There she would find her spirit rise,
On the gusts of heavens' winds.

As on her native mountain's ridges,
So upon God's solid word she'd stand.
From those lofty heights she'd view,
God's distant promise land.

No longer now is it from afar,
She does her home with Jesus see,
Today she with friends in heaven,
Will for evermore with Jesus be.

Dr. C.R. Hill, Jr.

## From the Trackless Wood Emerged

A faithful traveler on his way,
To heaven's promised home,
Late found himself in a trackless wood,
Unlike any he'd ever known.

It is hard to see the faithful ones,
Who had always led the way,
Have to take another's hand,
When near the end of day.

Yet God above does not forsake,
Though with eyes we may not see,
When the woods are dark and strange,
Ever present still is he.

Our traveler knew God's promise well,
So when he reached this trackless place,
He placed his hand in hands he loved,
And leaned on God's unchanging grace.

Even deep and trackless woods,
Have boundaries and an end,
So on he walked by faith alone,
With Jesus as his friend.

Now from this wood he has emerged,
In the light of God's great love,
And walked with Jesus all the way,
To his new home up above.

## Joyce's Song

There is a notion among us mortal folks,
That the blessed life is one of ease.
No pain of suffering is what we seek,
When in prayer upon our knees.

Yet Jesus shows us a different view,
Of what a victorious life is made.
Victory comes at our weakest points,
When we must fully trust God's aid.

To win the highest crown of life,
Is not to sail through life unscathed,
It is instead when in suffering's grip,
To endure it unafraid.

It is the trust from deep within,
In God's great promises so true,
That nothing earth and life can wrought,
That can take his love from you.

So our sister before us now,
Does at last her victory gain.
She endured through greatest strife,
A lion's share of pain.

Yet in it all no complaint she made,
Nor did she desert her faith in God,
But holding fast to Jesus' hand,
She to doubts gave not a nod.

Oh today she walks on streets of gold,
With loved ones at her side,
And sings her praise to Christ her king,
Who here suffered for her and died.

Dr. C.R. Hill, Jr.

## Come Home 'Preacher'

Come here preacher,
You see that land out there?
We'll build a church on it,
Line the roads with Bradford Pear.

Then over there,
Where stands that grove pine,
Two hundred families living safe,
Is the picture I have in mind.

Come here preacher,
There is so much more to see,
Don't just look at things the way they are,
And miss the way that they could be.

Otherwise you'll miss,
All the lives your life can reach.
Why, is not that the reason,
The Lord called you to preach?

Now listen brother,
The thing we must do is pray,
Then we'll just settle back;
Trust the Lord to have his way.

Come home, "Preacher",
You see that mansion there,
It is the house I had built for you,
The one that Jesus did prepare.

## Marching Orders Received

Another soldier receives the call,
As marching orders arrive,
From this campaign of strife and death,
To heaven where we'll always be alive.

Our great Commander and our Chief,
Has himself made for us the way.
He at port to welcome us,
On our eternal homecoming day.

Now our soldier his campaign won,
To his commander always true,
Receives the final crown of life,
As all God's faithful soldiers do.

The medals here on earth received,
Will be turned to rust with time,
But his crown of life in Christ his Lord,
Will throughout all the ages shine.

As for you who loved him here,
And are left to bid adieu,
Weep not long his marching on,
He has only marched ahead of you.

He will be waiting up ahead,
When your voyage of life is done,
And there to greet you at the port,
With your Savior, God's Own Son.

Dr. C.R. Hill, Jr.

## Whispers of Reveille

So once again to this hillside green,
We come bearing earthly clay,
For another soul has traveled home,
To await Reunion Day.

When last we came for such a cause,
'Twas with the child so long gone home,
'Tis today her mother's turn,
Who rich length of days has known.

Brief or long 'tis of little note,
Once the race of life is run,
Save in the latter case grows long,
The list of things they've done.

Yet when at last the taps are played,
The thing that counts comes down to one,
That on the path from birth to death,
One knew Jesus Christ God's Son.

In the daughter's case we know,
God never released the infant's hand,
Now mother too waits with her,
For she with Jesus took her stand.

Now the circle here has shrunk by one,
As taps mark the ending of her way,
Yet the distant echoes sound,
Whispers the reveille of Reunion Day.

## Until Reunion Day

In an earlier storm of life,
An infant came and went.
'Twas there some danger Jesus saw,
That he recalled the child he sent?

No doubt the time was just not right,
For her to begin her precious life,
The world she entered raged with war,
Her father was missing in the strife.

But a child recalled is never lost,
Just restored to the Father's home,
There they wait for earthly kin,
Before the heavenly Father's throne.

So now upon this hillside green,
Rest her tiny robe of clay,
But the child who wore it for a span,
Awaits with you reunion day.

Dr. C.R. Hill, Jr.

# The Homecoming

Now she comes to that heavenly home,
Though on earth she sojourned long,
Ever looking for that happy land,
Of joyful heavenly song.

Her life's love long before her gone,
She was restless here below,
She longed to gain the heavenly prize,
Reserved for those who Jesus know.

Yea now on heaven's golden streets,
She is walking straight and tall,
With shouts of joy and radiant smile,
She greets her loved ones all.

There she takes the outstretched hand,
Of the husband she on earth so loved,
As together they view the heavenly home,
Built for them by Jesus above.

Then down at Jesus' nail scarred feet,
She humbly bows on reverent knee,
To receive from him the crown of life,
That he bought on Calvary's tree.

## On the Crossing of Jordin

Two brothers, young, set out one day,
But for each other almost alone,
Little kindness did life show them,
They had no home to call their own.

Then one day a couple's path,
Did with theirs chance to intersect,
As they walked life's path with them,
They taught them love and self-respect.

It took some time and patience too,
For the one to get just what they taught,
That God the Father seeks souls like his,
For his heavenly home that Jesus bought.

Yet as the months and years went by,
That couple's message did sink in,
That his heavenly Father's love,
Had a special place for him.

O' far too soon for that couple's hearts,
Did he cross the river of his name,
But through the love they gave to him,
He did in Jesus a new home gain.

## I'll See You Again

Your family grew smaller by one today,
As your mother journeyed home.
Yet today around God's heavenly table,
Your family by one has grown.

Sadness fills your hearts I know,
You feel an empty place inside.
It is the void love leaves behind,
When a loved one here has died.

But God will never leave you thus,
With this vacant place unfilled,
Though now it feels like an ocean wide,
It is Jesus who the ocean stilled.

So shed the tears you must today,
And yes tomorrow too.
But as your tears of sorrow flow out,
Let God fill you with his joys anew.

Death on earth is a passing thing,
For all who here in Jesus trust.
In Jesus Christ one never dies,
Though leave from earth one must.

So let God fill that empty space,
That sad void so deep within,
With the assurance of his living hope,
Then Rejoice! You will see her once again.

## The Shadow of a Giant

A giant crossed the bar today;
He stands among us here no more.
He stepped across that crystal sea,
To walk through heaven's open door.

Slowly, sadly we watched him leave,
Though for us it still came too fast.
His giant presence we yet would wish,
Could here with us much longer last.

But he was ready his work here done,
His towering figure bent with pain,
He placed it all in his Savior's hands,
Then walked home with him to heaven gain.

Now there with those who have gone before,
His wife, his son and many others too,
He is dwelling today in Beulah Land,
Where God in Jesus makes all things new.

A legacy of faith he leaves behind,
As his lasting gift to you each one,
Hold fast the hand of Jesus Christ,
Then join him there when your race is run.

So shed the tears you must shed now,
For love demands it from your heart,
But sorrow's tears today will be joy's tomorrow,
When we gather there never more to part.

Dr. C.R. Hill, Jr.

# In the Father's Loving Palm

Sometimes a life finds easy seas,
With calm and gentle wind.
Sometimes the seas are rough with storms,
That seem bound to do us in.

While none would chose the storm to sail,
With its danger, fear, or loss,
The measure of a soul comes through,
When in the storms of life they toss.

The weaker souls give up at once,
In fear they cry and wail,
But those with temper in their steel,
Rise up to face the gale.

They do not curse the intruding storm,
Rather they steer to face the wind,
Then setting course on God's great love,
They sail across life's sea to him.

In faith they know the storms will pass,
And that there is a harbor safe and calm.
For they know whatever seas they sail,
That they are in the Father's loving palm.

To Walk in Heaven's Light
# Going By His Place

Before I knew the man,
I knew his place.
The yard was always filled,
With cords of wood.
Firewood—stacked in order,
Filling every space.

The kind of wood you'd use,
To stoke a warm-morning stove,
Or bring a cheerful glow,
From a friendly fireplace,
Or chase the winter chill,
From a country kitchen cove.

Not on their own,
Grew these cords of wood.
I felt I knew the man,
From going by his place.
I saw him in my mind working at his task,
Muscular and lean as with ax in hand he stood.

With large and calloused hands,
A rugged sort of chap,
Yet with heart so warm it glowed,
Like the embers that remain,
When evening logs have all but burned away,
To warm a welcome winter's nap.

I felt I knew the man,
From just going by his place.
And when in time the chance arose,
That we were introduced,
I felt as though we had long been friends,
When I met him face to face.

I then discovered he knew The Man,
From going by His place.
I could tell when I gripped his hand,
That the faith he had was strong,
And he'd be leaving with the friend he knew,
From going by his place.

165

Dr. C.R. Hill, Jr.

## Precious in God's Sight

From this land of pain and tears,
From this forest filled with fear,
To those pastures green and fresh,
Our loved one has gone from here.

Stumbling feet and stammering speech,
No longer can her life hold down,
Freed from all her fettered bonds,
She walks today where God's gifts abound.

'Tis from the cup of salvation full,
She drinks of God's eternal life,
While in God's mansion built for her,
Now waits for you your mother and wife.

So shed the tears of sorrow now,
'Tis love's demand when gone one's love,
But shed them in the joy of hope,
For you love endures in heaven above.

Then walk as she this path of earth,
As long as God still gives you breath,
And be assured by this path of Christ,
God delivers his saints from death.

## From Water's Edge to Heaven's Shore

It was by the water's edge,
That she spent most of her days,
Only in her autumn years,
Did she take on our midland ways.

Yet when she came to be with us,
In our town so far from shore,
It wasn't long before all fell in love,
With our precious Betty Moore.

Near twenty years have come and gone,
As to us she grew so dear.
Who would have known a week ago,
That her crossing time was near.

Now our hearts are grieved to know,
That from our town she's gone,
Back again to the water's edge,
And from there she has sailed home.

But we shall soon see her again,
On that eternal distant shore,
Where with Jesus we'll reunite,
And from dear ones part no more.

In the meantime as we look back,
On the path she took through life,
We'll note it was with Christ she walked,
Through all the trials of earthly strife.

Dr. C.R. Hill, Jr.

# Passing Through

She never really lived here,
Though she stayed here for a while,
And whenever her children spoke of her,
'Twas always with a smile.

Some people pass before their time,
When it seems they've just begun to live,
Others linger painfully long,
Having given all they have to give.

'Tis neither long or shorter days,
That measure life in time,
But what a life has impressed upon,
The lives it leaves behind.

So she's moved on away from here,
To a home she will adore.
There, husband Paul awaits for her,
Where they will live forever more.

And though she never really lived here,
And though we never really met,
She still has left her mark here,
For her children are smiling yet.

## The Master of Mended Souls

A simple shoe-man he was by trade,
A cobbler mending soles.
Yet a man of vision keen,
Who set his sights on higher goals.

It was as though he had inner eyes,
Quick to see what others missed,
And he set his life to touch other's eyes,
That they might experience vision's bless.

A man of courage unafraid to try,
With an adventurous kind of flair.
He made his way quite well in life,
Going where others would not dare.

And yet, in spite of his life's success,
He remained a humble, gentle man,
A man of kindly, gracious love,
Who firmly held God's hand.

Yes, a simple shoe-man he was by trade,
A cobbler mending soles,
Who understood that his Savior was,
The Master of mended souls.

Dr. C.R. Hill, Jr.

# On Heaven's Golden Street

When a body has breathed its last,
And closed in death these eyes of clay,
It then appears to us who yet remain,
That death has had the final say.

But that's a lie! It is not the truth,
For we who in Jesus have put our trust,
Know that life goes on in endless glory,
Though our earthly shell has gone to dust.

For Jesus Christ our great High Priest,
Has overcome for us the grave,
He has entered in the heavenly tent,
A place there for us to save.

Thus by our resurrected Lord,
We've been born to this living hope,
We know what is seen with earthly eyes,
Is not at all life's total scope.

In Jesus Christ the risen Lord,
Though our hearts are broken we yet rejoice
For through our tears and deepest sobs,
We still hear his reassuring voice.

He whispers to our soul's deep pain,
His eternal promises so sweet,
That with our loved one we will walk again,
On heaven's golden street.

## In The Life Beyond Tomorrow

Danny has stepped across the bar,
And from earth and sorrow he's gone,
Yet you who loved and felt for him,
Are left with sorrow to journey on.

There is a balm that can ease your pain,
And reclaim your heart from sorrow,
For God in Christ walks now with you,
To give you life beyond tomorrow.

In death's dread curse your place he took,
To wash clean your soul from sin,
And in heaven he's made a place for you,
So you can pass from death to life again.

Now behold he sends his Spirit's love,
To seal this gift he died to give,
For if you will trust and Christ obey,
Though you die you yet shall live.

So you who still here on earth remain,
Grieving for what might have been,
Draw near in faith to take God's hand,
And in his peace walk on with him.

Dr. C.R. Hill, Jr.

# Always Looking Up

His job upon the gridiron,
Was to get the quarterback,
He was always looking up,
For the way to make the sack.

Never when the play began,
Would he be looking down,
He knew that if he did,
He would end up on the ground.

Always when the ball was snapped,
He was looking up to find the way,
To get through all of the blockers,
And on the quarterback make the play.

You never saw him look around,
To first take care of number one;
He took a lot of hits that way,
Yet his aim was getting his job done.

Now by his life he has shown us,
That in the game of life to win,
We must keep on looking up to God,
And the way to play for him.

## Finally Home

"I'll be home for Christmas,"
Claims the old familiar line,
"I'll be home for Christmas,
If only in my *mind*."

Within the heart of each of us,
There is that special longing,
To spend the dearest hour of the year,
With the ones to us belonging.

Thus when those special people,
Stepped from time to Heaven's shore,
Then the season made for singing,
Feels not as festive any more.

But that is not as it should be,
Instead our songs should rise with joy;
For so we could enter Heaven,
God has sent us his baby boy.

So when a loved one passes from us,
Stepping beyond life's earthly page,
Life for them is hardly over,
It has just begun for endless age.

And when a loved one leaves at Christmas,
To go and stand before God's throne,
There is for truth no cause for sadness,
Because for Christmas they're finally home.

Dr. C.R. Hill, Jr.

# In the Resurrection Morning

We went down to the burial grounds,
To lay our dear one to rest,
There in the shadow of sadness,
My faith in my God I did test.

My spirit within me was weeping,
My beautiful dear one was gone,
But here in the place of life's ending,
I knew that my dear one lives on.

The place was the essence of stillness,
Not a soul did I see there alive,
But strangely in this place of deep quiet,
Started my faith in my God to thrive.

The tears on my face were still salty,
The ache in my heart brought its pain,
Yet, there in that garden of grave stones,
Began my hope in my Savior to reign.

Then joy within me was leaping,
My feet felt a strange urge to dance,
I knew Jesus has won us the victory,
So to hold us death has not a chance.

O the shadow of death is still with us,
And this graveyard still looks sound asleep,
But the morning of resurrection is coming,
When God his promise of life will keep.

Until then my dear one will not be here sleeping,
She will stand in God's presence and sing,
And the echo of her heavenly music,
Will meanwhile in my heart yet ring.

## A Father's Steps

A father's steps first mark the path,
That a child with love will trace,
And all the years won't from the heart,
Those early steps of love erase.

Years will pass as the child does grow,
To forge pathways of their own,
Yet the trail they leave reflects the course,
That the father's steps have shown.

The child one day becomes a man,
Or a woman true and proud,
Yet it is the father's early steps,
That helps set them above the crowd.

Now Dad has gone, by his latter steps,
He's left the paths of earth we've known,
To trace toward heaven the Father's steps,
Along the path that Christ has shown.

So as we walk on along the paths of time,
Let us in our hearts walk on with him,
And trace with Jesus our Father's steps,
Until we in heaven meet again.

Dr. C.R. Hill, Jr.

## Born to Rise Eternal

A time is set for every soul,
To this earthly journey end,
Then go on to a brighter realm,
If while here they were born again.

For Jesus did from heaven come,
To bring new birth for every soul,
Who would in faith receive him in,
And make heaven their life's goal.

Now to us the time has come,
For our dear one to take his flight,
From the days of darkness aging brings;
To God's golden realm of light.

He lived in faith his life below,
Showing love through healing hands,
Now the legacy he leaves behind,
Before us in honor stands.

May all who knew him through his years,
Mark well his footprints on this earth,
Then set their hearts to live as him,
By finding in Christ the second birth.

## The Voice of the Morning Breeze

Oh give me the wings of the morning,
Let me soar with the morning breeze,
I'll take my leave of this weary world,
With a body no pain can seize.

I would tarry longer here below,
For the love I have known is dear,
But the morning breeze is calling to me,
And God's heavenly love draws me near.

Oh think me not so far away,
Though the days be lonely or long,
I'll caress your cheek with the morning breeze,
And warm your heart with the word of a song.

I'll hover above on the morning breeze,
Keeping watch as the days go by,
Until that day you spread your wings,
And soar through the morning sky.

Dr. C.R. Hill, Jr.

# By the Christmas Baby's Voice

The Christmas sights are fading here,
The lights have all grown dim.
I am ready now to leave it all,
And spend Christmas there with him.

These packages beneath the tree,
All wrapped so fancily,
Hold not the magic I desire,
That can from my prison set me free.

My feeble legs can't hold me up,
The children's laughter I can't hear.
I've gone to hear Christmas Angels sing,
All throughout the year.

The Tree of Life I'll there behold,
I'll touch the Christmas Baby's face,
I'll bask this year and forever more,
In the light of God's redeeming grace.

O children dear weep not for me,
Nor let my leaving mute your joy.
I've simply gone to spend Christmas now,
With the manger's Baby Boy.

I am singing now with the angel choirs,
In heaven's glorious light,
For from this weary prison on earth,
I have with Jesus taken flight.

So you my children sing all the more,
In the Christmas news rejoice!
Tune your ears throughout your years,
To hear the Christmas Baby's voice.

178

## The Home Jesus Built Above

A homesick soul is well today,
Her journey on earth complete.
The joys and sorrows of life behind,
Today she is singing at Jesus' feet.

Oh she had her fun while here with you,
With her pranks and tomboy schemes.
She could throw a perfect spiral pass,
And fill her children's hearts with dreams.

The joy of music sprang from her hands,
When her fingers met the keys,
And heaven's wave notes filled her heart,
When before Jesus she bowed her knees.

Yet for all the joy of life she'd known,
She found life's final hills quite hard to climb,
And longed she did for that higher plane,
Where she with her husband again would dine.

So with the joys of her life all packed,
In your memory's treasure chest,
She has taken her leave of earth,
And laid this earthly tent of clay to rest.

Today in heaven she dances glad and free,
With him who was through life her love,
And there with him she peace has found,
In the home Jesus built for them above.

Dr. C.R. Hill, Jr.

## With the Master Pilot

For one final flight he long prepared,
Though not anxious to depart,
Still he held no fear of what lay ahead,
Once he would his journey start.

He flew on many missions,
In the wars of earth he fought.
And he'd met the Master Pilot,
Found the peace this pilot brought.

For a lifetime now together,
Both of them have flown,
The Master Pilot his instructor,
Has the ways of life made known.

They've now taxied down the runway,
The wheels lifted from the ground,
For a home above the clouds of earth,
The two of them are bound.

There before the Master Pilot,
He will bow on bended knee,
Then soaring throughout the heavens,
With the Master Pilot he will be.

## The Passing of a Lady

A lady passed away today,
And made her journey home.
Unescorted by friends of earth,
She made the trip alone.

Her friends of earth are sad today,
For her death to them is loss.
Yet for her sake we here rejoice,
That she's safely gone across.

'Twas without regret she took her leave,
Though she was not in haste to go.
She knew her time had run its course,
As she left her house below.

In heaven today those pearly gates,
Are surely opened wide,
And an angel band strikes up a tune,
As our lady struts inside.

And there to greet her by the throne,
Among a throng of friends,
Are Momma, Brother, and Christ her lord,
With whom life never ends.

Dr. C.R. Hill, Jr.

## Friends with a Saint

A saint was laid to rest today.
His friends on earth saw him on his way.

His friends above were standing by,
To show him to his home on high.

Blessed the man with peace unknown.
Who has friends in death to see him home.

His friends of earth who watch him leave,
Surely mark their loss and pause to grieve.

But the streets of heaven resound with joy,
As friends above say, "hello" to Roy.

There are bulldogs there he'll have to tease,
And children gathered at his knees.

Then his crown cast down at Jesus' throne,
For heaven he gained by this friend alone.

## Heaven's Summer Garden Room

Winter is waning on our hill,
Of windswept yard and trees.
Warmer days are drawing near,
But I'll leave you to enjoy these.

I've seen enough of winter days,
I've felt all I wish her icy chill,
I've taken leave of earth's harsh pain,
To climb up heaven's summer hill.

I'd love to stay a longer while,
To see spring change the earth again,
But winter has worn this body out,
I'm going to rest in heaven's den.

There summer's season never ends,
There blow not death's icy winds.
When seasons on the earth are done,
God's summer season just begins.

So watch the waning winter sky,
Soon behold the dogwoods bloom.
Then remember that I with Jesus am,
In heaven's summer garden room.

Dr. C.R. Hill, Jr.

## Measure Twice, Saw Once

Learn to use this ruler son,
You'll find it a faithful friend,
Measure twice, saw but once,
Things will fit right in the end.

Measure twice, saw but once,
Think it through before you act,
Once the saw has made its slice,
It's too late to take it back.

Learn to use my ruler child,
I hear my Heavenly Father say,
Let the measure of the life you build,
Match with my perfect way.

Thus it was he measured life,
Not to earthly rulers scale,
But by the master builder's grace,
He built a home within God's veil.

Jesus whispers down once more,
These words I can't forget,
Measure twice, saw but once,
And your life with mine will fit.

## Grieve Not My Love

We have come my dear,
Too soon to the parting ways.
The years have sped so quickly by,
They seem only several days.

Now our Lord has summoned me,
Though I wished to be with you.
My time on earth has run its course,
The race I've run is through.

Grieve not my love, nor be afraid,
Though our Lord has called me home,
Jesus promised, now I clearly see,
You are not in the least alone.

Why, I see angels attending you,
They stand at your feet and head,
And He who holds your trembling hand,
Is the resurrection from the dead.

It is okay to shed your tears,
But in sorrow do not despair,
Why glorious things were shown to me,
When my spirit did part the air.

Dear, you will come safely through,
Though the way is steep right now,
For every step I'll take with you,
Until you too before God bow.

185

Dr. C.R. Hill, Jr.

# A Name That Stood For More

See that building on the square.
His name is above the door.
No merchant he whose store it was,
That name stood for something more.

A quiet man of humble grace,
Who judged with justice rare,
Respect of all who knew the man,
Was what put his name up there.

Justice was at home with him,
And he with justice too,
He sought in every part of life,
That which was right to do.

Humble also describes him well,
He had no illusions of himself,
I met him not in a judge's robe,
But as he dusted my bookshelf.

But love is the word that fit him best,
Love for family, friends and land,
Love for Jesus and his Church,
And lives precious in God's hand.

See that building on the square,
With his name above the door,
It is there to say to passersby,
"Life counts for something more."

## Around the Last Corner

Strange how the roads we must travel,
Meander through many a turn.
In youth for adventures we hunger,
By evening for heaven we yearn.

In the morning our strength seems unfailing,
Forever we feel we can run.
By sunset we've used all our powers,
As for adventures, we appear to be done.

Yet the spirit is not easily finished,
Though the body has made its last turn,
The heart that has traveled with Jesus,
For adventures continues to yearn.

Nor is the yearning to be easily quieted,
Though breath to lungs is all gone,
For the spirit unfettered and earthbound,
Life's greatest adventure is on.

So weep for me but for a moment,
And whatever befalls don't despair,
When your spirit rounds its last corner,
With Jesus I'll be waiting there.

Dr. C.R. Hill, Jr.

## The Model Man

When you grow up all straight and tall,
And you a man become to be,
I'd like to think that you've become,
A man the likes of he.

In him a man of stature tall.
I've often chanced to see,
In him a man of gentle ways,
And sure integrity.

When you grow up to your full height,
And take your place with men,
I'd like to think you've become,
The man I've seen in him.

For he's a man to point the way,
For younger men like you,
A man whose life I worthy deem,
To be a model man that's true.

This model man has left us now,
To take up his home above,
But the world he leaves behind for us,
Is much better for his love.

Yet our life on earth is brief at best,
Soon we must take our place,
Among such noble model folks,
If we too, the Master's footsteps trace.

## Taking Flight with the Autumn Leaves

Little Doc took flight from earth,
On a mid-October morn,
As autumn leaves began to turn,
He made his journey home.

He watched the seasons come and go,
For almost four score years,
And while we are sad to bid farewell,
We can mix laughter with our tears.

Oh, Little Doc did enjoy life!
He knew how to fill each day with fun,
But he also looked to that better home,
Built for him by God's dear son.

So the office door is long since closed,
And his smile has left the room,
But we know that we will see him there,
When we in heaven our life resume.

For when his leaves of life had turned,
And had set in life's winter chill,
He took his leave to be with God,
Where for life it's springtime still.

Dr. C.R. Hill, Jr.

## On the Wings of God

I girded on the spirit's wind,
Just as other souls took flight.
And I was drawn to soar with them,
To ever rising height.

I saw the clouds of earth roll back,
Like a window in the sky,
And through its opened sash they flew,
To meet the Lord on high.

I longed to see through those parted clouds,
To glimpse heaven's celestial sea.
As on they flew, those rising souls,
Who soared ahead of me.

Beyond the window of parting clouds,
I could glimpse a glorious sight,
And those who flew ahead of me,
Were enveloped in heaven's light.

I sought to follow where they'd gone,
To bask in heaven's "son",
"But I was bid to return to earth
Until I my course did run."

'Twas only then that I did learn,
Dorothy Ray was one of those,
Soaring that morning ahead of me,
As on the spirit's wings we rose.

## Sitting Delighted at God's Table

I recall an evening scene,
As the supper meal was done,
When his dad took Joe to his room,
I saw the love of this father for his son.

Now as I reflect upon that scene,
New insight fills my eyes.
It speaks to me of the love and grace,
That our heavenly Father supplies.

We're all as needy as was Joe;
We are all no sharper or more able,
To help ourselves, or be deserving,
Of a place at God's heavenly supper table.

Yet as this family with patient love,
Assured that Joe always had a place,
At the table and in their hearts,
So are we the debtors to God's grace.

Surely God sent Joe into this family,
So we who knew them could discern,
How God through Jesus for us provides,
An eternal hope we could not earn.

Just as his dad helped Joe that night,
To the room love did provide,
So Jesus has for each of us prepared,
A place we can with him forever reside.

O' we can now each rest assured,
That Joe is sitting alert and bright,
At the family's heavenly table,
His face aglow with pure delight.

Dr. C.R. Hill, Jr.

# A Chat on Heaven's Porch

Come my dear, sit here awhile,
Your long dark night is ended.
It is time to rest in the Father's house,
With the Christ whom you befriended.

O I've been waiting by yonder gate,
To walk you up this lane,
So we could sit here on heaven's porch,
And be together once again.

No, the view from here does not look back,
On the hardships you've come through.
It looks instead on pastures green,
With God's promises so true.

'Twas a test back there, those painful things,
And your faith has overcome,
From here on out we'll dine each day,
With Jesus, God's first Son.

With him, too, we'll share all things,
For his grace has made us whole.
His life, his death, and life again,
Has made this home to house our soul.

O' they'll be coming who remain behind,
If they too shall choose to come,
For he has cleared the path for them,
And treasures each and every one.

But come now dear for just inside,
The others wait to welcome you,
Your room's prepared, the banquet's spread,
Now God makes all things brand new.

## Her Gold Refined

Our course in life does often lead,
Down paths we'd rather shun,
'Tis then the tempter calls to us,
"Now turn your back and run."

That the urge is strong is not denied,
When we are at a loss to know the why,
Confused and feeling all alone,
We hang our head and cry.

Yet all alone we never are,
For God does never our side leave,
All he asks is when our light is gone,
For us to in his light believe.

He will never let a single thing,
To his plan for us defeat.
It is at our weakest point in life,
That he makes his power in us complete.

So it was for this loved one dear,
At whose leaving we're so grieved,
The fires of life have refined her gold,
Now she has her eternal crown received.

Dr. C.R. Hill, Jr.

## The Crown through Jesus Won

We have learned again the other day,
What a fragile gift is life.
We've seen anew the senseless way,
It is snatched away amid earth's strife.

Once again we've been made aware,
Of how precious is our jar of clay,
And how important it is to make,
Every moment count along our way.

For in the end it is not by length,
That the measure of life we take,
For one will laugh at time to come,
Who does on Jesus the victory stake.

Yea, in pursuit of the ultimate prize,
For which the race of life is run,
One need not fear the early finish,
Who has the crown through Jesus won.

## His View from Above the Clouds

As hot air carries a balloon aloft,
To vistas wide and grand,
So too are human souls raised up,
By the power of Jesus' hand.

From his gondola among the clouds,
He viewed the earth that Jesus made;
Then he took an upward glance,
At the home he'd reach with Jesus' aid.

It is not today from a gondola perch,
Or with a glance towards heaven's goal,
That he now views his heavenly home,
Because Jesus saved his soul.

O' he walks today on golden streets,
As angels their anthems sing,
Then bows before that glorious throne,
Where Jesus reigns forever as the king.

It is ok to take some time,
To mourn the fact that he has gone,
But then let joy replace your tears,
As closer to Jesus you are drawn.

Then in the promise you too one day,
Will on those golden highways stroll,
And as while still on earth you live,
Make Jesus your heart's goal.

Dr. C.R. Hill, Jr.

## On Silent Wings He Flew

At the wonder of God's world,
He would for hours contemplate,
All the marvels of God's grace,
In his mind he would debate.

First hand he saw God's grace at work,
When certain death he faced at sea,
Until God cleared the fog away,
For crew and pilots to rejoice with glee.

Through the years on silver wings,
He'd cross and cross again the skies,
He'd count the stars and search for lights,
As he filled God's ears with a thousand "Whys."

Spellbound he was by one great truth,
That a sinner such as was he,
Could dare to hope for the chance,
To know God's love and heaven see.

Yet as a pilot to a carrier deck,
Must surrender control and to it commit,
So to the arms of Jesus he did trust,
As to God's salvation he did submit.

Then while others lay in racks asleep,
Or keep the watches before the dawn,
On silent wings from the deck above,
He took his flight and from us was gone.

## Home by the Higher Way

I met a traveler of the higher way,
That winds its way through life,
And leads the soul to higher planes,
Despite life's trials and strife.

Life's upward and life's downward trails,
Can often close parallels run,
In times of the soul's distress,
They can sometimes appear as one.

'Tis the soul that calls which way will go,
To life's planes of praise and light,
By whether one should choose to walk,
As toward God or endless night.

'Twas truly the upward way she trod,
Though it had parallel run with strife,
For she had fixed her hopes on God,
And chosen his way to endless life.

She now has come by that highway home,
Today she is walking on heaven's sod.
And the higher way she traveled here,
Will us, too, lead home to God.

Dr. C.R. Hill, Jr.

## The Christ-Learned Way

A quiet witness took his flight,
As night turned into day.
This man who dared to live his faith,
And walk the Christ-learned way.

He never served a mega church.
No silk tie preacher he.
He served where glamour never walked,
And where others feared to be.

His voice was never deep and loud,
He was of small and delicate frame;
Yet faith has known no brighter light,
Who bore more proudly Jesus' name.

In life on earth he lingered long,
Well past life's joys and health.
Though we viewed him weak and poor,
He drew joys from his heavenly wealth.

This quiet witness has taken flight,
From earth's night to heaven's day,
And in the example he left for us,
May we, too, walk the Christ-learned way.

## Anchors for the Soul

Some days in life are crystal clear,
With sun filled skies so bright,
Some days bring the raging storms,
That seem to bring us endless night.

So are the days when loved ones die,
We are like ships driven by a gale,
Afraid that against the waves of grief,
Our ship of life cannot prevail.

Yet when upon our raging sea,
We lift up our hearts and pray,
We find some anchors that will hold,
Until God's new approaching day.

There is the anchor of God's help,
Walking beside us through the storms,
And when we feel we cannot go on,
We find he carries us in his arms.

The anchor too of hope we have,
Not some sentimental wish,
But the promise of the one who fed,
Five thousand with just two fish.

A home he promised to build for us,
On heaven's eternal ground,
Then come to take us to himself,
That we ever with him be found.

This honor is our final stay,
An anchor in our control,
To live in ways upon this earth,
That will honor our loved one's soul.

199

Dr. C.R. Hill, Jr.

## Beyond Autumn's Clear Blue Sky

As trees shed their gowns of gold,
'Neith autumn's clear blue sky,
A saint has shed the robes of earth,
And spread her wings to fly.

O' like the mighty forest oaks,
Or a stately ridge-top pine,
She spent her years upon this earth,
Living out her Lord's design.

Yet, as it is with all living things,
That the Lord God placed on earth,
There is an allotted time that fills,
The space 'twix death and birth.

With the oak its measure is its rings,
The pine how tall it's grown.
With us it's the shadow that we've cast,
Upon everyone we've known.

Now she has gone with the golden leaves,
And ascended autumn's clear blue skies,
Yet her shadow lingers upon your hearts,
As she receives her heavenly prize.

## One by One on Heaven's Shore

One by one they leave our planet,
To join the church victorious up above.
One by one their suffering ended,
They bask forever in heaven's love.

Now our brother here remembered,
Has shed the chains of earthly woe,
So we should not let sorrow prevail,
Though for a season tears must flow.

With his race of life now finished,
He runs today on streets of gold,
Long ago he claimed God's promise,
Of life in Christ that grows not old.

Fewer now are here this morning,
As one by one your ranks decrease,
But oh the joy that in heaven awaits you,
For James has now their ranks increased.

Your path from here is not unfamiliar,
And though he is gone you are not alone.
For God in Jesus walks beside you,
As you keep from here his pathway home.

So let God's promise of life eternal,
Day by day restore and lift your soul,
Soon dawns the day for you to follow,
And like the others gain heaven's goal.

Dr. C.R. Hill, Jr.

# A Step from Time to Heaven Go

She fought to finish out the year with us,
 Yet for midnight she could not wait,
 For on this special New Year's Eve,
 She had a very special date.

 When the Ball at Times Square fell,
 And in Atlanta the Peach did drop,
 She was seated at the table,
Where clocks never more will stop.

 Good years among us she did live,
 And hard ones too close to the end.
 Now years to her mean not a thing,
With year's end life eternal did begin.

 Yet it was not then entirely so,
That New Year's brought eternal life.
Long she has known that faith in Christ,
 Always lifts one above time's strife.

 It was while living with us in time,
That eternal life she had come to know.
So on New Year's Eve the only change,
Was she stepped from time to heaven go.

202

## In the Hymns of Hope and Heaven

Heaven just got sweeter,
Another saint has just gone home,
She was one of the finest,
That this earth has ever known.

She leaves behind a canyon,
In our lives who carry on,
Not believing that she's taken,
Feeling empty that she's gone.

Yet yonder blooms a Jonquil,
Like one she once did paint,
And there in a piece of driftwood,
We still see her image faint.

A bird flutters in a treetop,
A Monarch Butterfly floats by,
Then we see her smiling softly,
In a sunset painted sky.

And when we cross the churchyard,
At our favorite gathering spot,
In the hymns of hope and heaven,
We feel she has really left us not.

So instead of tearful partings,
We will choose to say good night,
For we will see her in the morning,
Of God's eternal day so bright.

Dr. C.R. Hill, Jr.

## In Heaven with Her Pilot

The angel on his wing,
Do we now know just who she is,
The spirit of the bride he loved,
Who now in heaven with him lives?

Her spirit rode with him through danger,
She walked with him through sorrow,
Now together they are waltzing,
In God's promised bright tomorrow.

Beyond this world which she had painted,
On canvas scenes so bright,
Beyond the roses of her walkway,
Where she sculpted budding life.

She now strolls God's golden highway,
Beside the river from his throne,
There she receives the Savior's welcome,
As she enters heaven's home.

There all the sorrows that she carried,
All the pain she knew on earth,
Has been changed to heaven's treasure,
The jewels of life's eternal worth.

At the throne of God now bowing,
In great gratitude and praise,
She there with her loving pilot,
Will spend forever heaven's days.

## In Heaven's Pastures Green

Rich was her life in deeds of love,
And faithful service rendered,
To God from whom she drew her life,
As well as all his love would send her.

We often wonder with one so true,
Why God so long their night sustains,
But even through the darkest hours,
We find His grace with us remains.

Then when we see life from heaven's side,
Where time knows no bound or place,
It does the pain of the waiting night,
From all our earthly years erase.

By righteous paths from beyond our time,
She has with God a walk now taken,
For today by heaven's waters still,
She did from her long night awaken.

There with loved ones gone on before,
And with the grandson she'd not seen,
She will be waiting for each of you,
When you reach heaven's pastures green.

Dr. C.R. Hill, Jr.

# Crossing the Silver Tide

The storm is passing now,
The worst is all behind,
With the morning's coming,
God's Son will on you shine.

He'll take you by the hand,
And across the silver tide,
You'll walk with him in joy,
To in heaven's home abide.

The quiet steady way you lived,
Among us here below,
Leaves for us welcome wake,
That shows us the way to go.

Your devotion to your friends,
For God your faithful love,
Bespoke to all of a disciple's life,
That followed Jesus Christ above.

Now you've crossed the silver tide,
Sorrow and pain you've all resigned.
Walk on with Jesus to God's throne,
And your heavenly treasure find.

## The Reunion

Back from the far horizon,
Still just beyond our view,
Stinson is waiting, Mildred,
Waiting there for you.

God called him on before you,
Some errand he must fulfill,
You tarried here without him,
Trusting in your Father's will.

Long has been your waiting,
Steep the road you climb,
Now waiting days have ended,
Today you reach the heights sublime.

There to greet you is your Stinson,
And you'll go hand and hand,
To the mansion God's made ready,
Built upon his promised land.

Dr. C.R. Hill, Jr.

## Beyond the Far Horizon

Beyond the far horizon,
Beyond the distant hill,
The Father's house is waiting,
Where the saints are living still.

And to that lofty vision,
His heart of clay aspired.
His spirit was full of victory,
Though his flesh was faint and tired.

Among the huddled masses,
He once walked these valleys low,
Then Jesus lightly touched him,
And with Christ he longed to go.

He shunned the strong temptation,
To in the valley be content,
And beyond the far horizon,
When Jesus beaconed, Stinson went.

## From Better Jesus Knowing

She cheated death more times than one.
When everyone thought that she was gone,
She rose up saying, "Don't deal me out,
I plan to still keep living on."

Live on she did in a greater sense,
Than she ever had before,
For she responded saying, "Do come in."
The day Jesus knocked upon her door.

Too weak all thought she surely was,
To keep working at a daily job,
Yet she refused to let sickness win,
Or her from the joy of working rob.

She dove into the word of God,
In rich fellowship with others,
Women with whom she weekly met,
Some older, some still younger mothers.

It was in that group she drew new life,
And the strength to keep on going,
They were why she kept cheating death,
They, and from Jesus better knowing.

Dr. C.R. Hill, Jr.

## Going on in the Greatness of Grace

Gone now he is,
Passed beyond earth's troubled plain,
Yet, in his final hours here,
He caught heaven's upward train.

In his final parting hours,
He reached up in faith his hand,
And caught the downward reaching grasp,
Of the very Son of Man.

The nail prints there upon the palm,
He knew had been for him,
The angry wound upon the side,
He knew had washed away his sin.

So like the dying thief that day,
Who on the cross took Jesus in,
He too by grace has heaven gained,
And in Christ will live again.

Yet we who stay when loved ones pass,
Must still trace the path of tears,
The broken dreams and might have beens,
Of all the bygone years.

But don't despair in your hour of grief,
For grace awaits you too today,
The same forgiveness that brought him peace,
Can wash all your sorrows away.

## A Ransomed Spirit's Prayer

All are called from wayward paths,
By his voice for each unique,
Unto the way that leads to life,
If they will the way of Jesus seek.

Now our dear one travels on,
For she this upward way did find,
When to Jesus and his grace,
She did her heart resign.

In that way she walked a while,
While still with us on earth.
Now she's moved into the home,
She gained by heavenly birth.

It's fitting that imperfect folks,
For us should lead the way,
They call for us to follow Christ,
When from life's way we stray.

The countless ways here below,
All lead to death and strife.
Only the way of Jesus Christ,
Will lead one to endless life,

It was love, led her to find,
That way amid life's maze.
Now for you to walk it too,
Her ransomed spirit prays.

Dr. C.R. Hill, Jr.

## The Heavenly Voyager

Another soul has grasped God's hand,
And stepped across the veil,
A ship at harbor ready made,
Has anchor weighed and sailed.

From out beyond the realm of earth,
Has come orders from on high,
To leave behind the house of clay,
And rise where spirits never die.

Thus this Voyager has passed from earth,
And heaven's ranks increased,
His battle o'er his victory won,
Now his spirit rests in peace.

Hence, you who knew and loved him most,
This quiet, gentle man,
Need not despair as with no hope,
For Christ with you doth stand.

And Jesus dries all earthly tears,
Until you, too, shall heaven win.
Then in that light beyond the veil,
You'll see your Voyager yet again.

## In Celebration of Life

I watched her come to her journey's end,
Where her path wound down to the sea.
She paused there for a moment,
Then she bid farewell to me.

O we walked together for seventy years,
As content as two peas in a pod.
But as so often it is at the end of the way,
One stays behind, and one goes to God.

I'll miss her for sure, more than life itself,
For apart for these years we've not been,
But it is not very far to the end of my trail,
Then we'll be back together again.

All of our years we've been building for this,
On the foundation of our faith in our Lord,
And a mansion in heaven is waiting for us,
Secured forever by God's word.

So if my grief appears to be not very deep,
It is because for God's new day I can not wait.
I am not here today to weep over a death –
It is life eternal I here celebrate.

Dr. C.R. Hill, Jr.

## A Kinsman of the King

Who am I, someone has asked,
By what shall I be known?
My name, my race, the job I do,
Or by Christ upon his throne?

I would answer Christ at once,
But would I then be answering true?
Would that answer have an honest ring,
In light of all the things I do?

Who am I? I ask myself,
As before my looking glass I stand,
Do I define myself with false IDs,
The labels given me by man?

O grant me Lord an honest heart,
And a desire for a name that's true,
That when others look they need not ask,
They'll just know that I belong to you.

Was this a prayer that Ray had prayed?
If so then Jesus must have heard,
For looking now at the life he lived,
He was a clear reflection of God's word.

214

## His Spirit Sought the Sky

He'd been too long upon the ground,
For a man who lived to fly.
Earthbound his body may have been,
But his spirit sought the sky.

So upon that chilly night,
Beneath winter's waning moon,
He shed the shell of clay he'd worn,
Then flew to heaven's ready room.

O' we waited at the gate with him,
As his departure time drew near.
And he lingered there a little while,
With the ones he loved so dear.

But soon he heard the boarding call,
And he answered it with joy,
For the battle of his life was won,
Now to heaven he would deploy.

The passage for his flight was bought,
On Mount Calvary long ago,
So with his Savior flying at his side,
Off to heaven Rick did go.

Dr. C.R. Hill, Jr.

# God's Eternal Living Game

I remember David's Dad,
Jesse was his name,
I recall the love he had,
For a sandlot baseball game.

I recall when Jessie passed,
After years of aging pain,
How we laid him down to rest,
In the hope we'd meet again,

Now David too is gone from us,
In an instant like a flash,
And we're reminded that at its best,
Life here passes far too fast.

Yet life on earth is just a practice,
For God's eternal living game,
Played by those who live by faith,
In Jesus the Savior's name.

So David has left the practice field,
And with Jessie he plays again,
In hopes that all who loved them here,
Will through Jesus heaven win.

## The Doorway to God's Best

No grief there is upon the earth,
Like a mother's lonesome sorrow,
When the child she bore and raised,
Goes first to God's tomorrow.

No word there is, no human voice,
Can her mournful spirit lift.
The only solace sufficient then,
Is God's own precious gift.

The gift he gives of present love,
That walks in empathizing grace.
For God's heart has ached as yours,
As he's been walking in your place.

To this he adds his gift of peace,
From beyond the reach of man.
The reassuring peace within,
That the world can't understand.

Oh, once the mother of our Lord,
Did weep as now you do,
But Jesus rose to live again,
And in him, your child will too.

So go ahead and grieve for now,
A mother's love can do no less.
But, don't despair, 'tis not the end,
It is but the doorway to God's best.

Dr. C.R. Hill, Jr.

# At Heaven's Open Door

"I am ready now.
This time I must go home.
Though I know not how,
God won't let you walk alone."

"Don't talk that way.
You're going to be alright."
Her eyes gave her away,
She was going home that night.

"I've come too close before,
My life is in Jesus' hand,
I see heaven's open door—
Look! With you I see him stand."

Peace then lit her face,
As of heaven's parting child,
With grace she finished well her race,
Now on Christ she looked and smiled.

With courage stood the man,
Her parting hurt him so.
Then firmly grasping Jesus' hand,
He let his dear one go.

At heaven's open door they stood,
And she was going in.
"I am ready now." He understood,
Meant, "Until we meet again."

## In Heaven's Arms

Heaven opens wide her arms,
To welcome home each lamb,
Who walking through this life below,
Held firmly to God's hand.

Still he leads in pastures green,
And beside the waters still,
Those who linger here below,
Who live to do his will.

So it was in quiet faith,
He lived out his earthly days.
Seeking in God's pastures green,
On God's richest grace to graze.

When the valley grew dark and cold,
As the walls of death closed in,
No dread or fear possessed his soul,
For Jesus walked with him.

Now to brighter days he comes,
In heaven's glorious light,
For he did faithfully hold God's hand,
Throughout life's long dark night.

Dr. C.R. Hill, Jr.

# The Captain's Voyage

The Captain put to sea today,
His voyage comes as no surprise.
His ship has at the ready lay,
For the command from beyond the skies.

And though his sailing we have expected,
Its time's arrival leaves us sad,
For his companionship with us here,
Has been among the best we ever had.

His brave refusal to give in to death,
His ever determined pushing on.
Where others would have given up,
Makes us want also to be strong.

But not with the strength of human health,
In bodies fit and stable,
His was the strength of faith alone,
That in God's power did keep him able.

He showed us all what God can do,
When to Jesus one trusts their soul.
And now by always pushing on,
He has set sail for heaven's goal.

Yes, the captain put to sea today,
For like a captain he was to all,
As he led many to God's saving grace,
By having them on Jesus call.

## Before the Crystal Sea

'Tis bittersweet when a mother dies,
At an age advanced in years,
Though her trials of life are over,
One cannot hold back the tears.

The head knows well a better place,
Has now become her home,
Yet longs the heart to hear her voice,
When the hand picks up the phone.

Or on days when questions come to mind,
That one would always take to her,
And one finds oneself about to call,
'Tis then her absence is felt for sure.

Yet the bitter pain of missing her,
Finds joy mixed in the tears,
The memories of her special care,
Grows sweeter with passing years.

So to the joy one anticipates,
When once again her face we see,
Gathered 'round the throne of God,
Before the crystal sea.

Dr. C.R. Hill, Jr.

## Forever at Christmas Home

He was glad, I know he was,
To be near a daughter's love.
But no place could ever be like home,
Since his Maxine had gone above.

He kept the house they both had shared,
As long as did age and health permit,
But alas he could no longer stay,
So moved then our Jimmy Stitt.

And though the care was very good,
With some family so close by,
His heart was longing for that home,
God had built him in the sky.

It was that desire he shared with me,
Nearly every time we met.
He could not the reason understand,
God had not called him home as yet.

I am sure God had his reasons.
But who can know the things as such,
Could it have simply been because,
That home still needed Maxine's touch?

No matter now for Jimmy is gone.
He has not this Christmas spent alone,
For God has called and now he is there,
With her, forever at Christmas, home!

## The Artist's Hands

The artist's hands have paused to rest,
Her sculpture now complete.
The teacher has the class dismissed,
To go sit at the master carver's seat.

Her chalices are fully fired,
Their glaze long since applied,
She watches now the master work,
As she stands at his right side.

Yet her masterpieces here remain,
Not just in bowls of clay,
But in the lives of all she taught,
Along her lengthy way.

Some are bankers or doctors, too,
And some —why, teachers they became,
Yet each still bears her potter's mark,
Inscribed beneath their name.

'Tis in those vessels of human clay,
That her legacy is found,
And since she lost herself in them,
Jesus now adorns her with her crown.

Dr. C.R. Hill, Jr.

## Moved Home

"I am going home!"
These words, emphatic, clear, and strong,
Are the last I remember hearing,
Spoken by Grace Strawn.

"I am going home!"
No cause for mortal tears,
Home was where her heart was,
For all her earthly years.

Home meant mother and daddy,
And a family with whom she sang.
Home was a loving husband,
And where children's laughter rang.

But home means more than bricks and rafters,
Or familiar smells or sounds.
Home means also ever after,
Where the love of God abounds.

"I am going home!" No hesitation.
That was where she longed to be,
As she spoke somehow I knew,
She had in mind eternity.

"Home!"
She said it with a smile,
That told me she approved.
So when they told me Grace had died,
I knew she simply had moved Home!

## The Candy Man's Gone Home

Heaven's ranks increased today,
Swelled by yet another son,
Another saint from earth went home,
His life's victory finally won.

The way he walked while here below,
Was pure, good and sweet.
His golden crown he has now received,
To lay down at Jesus' feet.

On earth he sowed a garden fair,
Not just of beans and yams,
He sowed seeds of righteous living,
By teaching God's commands.

Today he travels heaven's street,
And beholds God's fertile fields,
Where grow the fruits of every life,
That to Jesus' Spirit yields.

O earth is a better place today,
For this saint before God's throne,
And heaven's ranks are increased by one,
For the "Candy Man"'s gone home.

Dr. C.R. Hill, Jr.

## He Lives

"It is finished", and all too soon,
Drew's little life is gone.
Like a candle through the darkest night,
That fades with braking dawn.

Oh, how our hearts did ache for him,
And how we wish it were not so,
That he could not with us longer be;
That so soon he had to go.

Yet, through that dark and fleeting night,
As his little life did shine,
He reached far beyond all walls,
And touched many hearts like mine.

He lead us to a depth of life,
We never knew we had,
And though it hurts to let him go,
For his coming we are glad.

He taught us how to rely on love,
Through every moment that we're given,
That life is measured by how we live,
And not how long we're liven.

"It is finished", and though too soon,
Drew's little life is gone,
He did leave before we knew,
That his little life lives on.

## Semper Fi, Always Faithful

The Leatherneck, the steel-trap mind,
The heart as big as all outdoors,
The gain belongs to heaven now,
While the loss is mine and yours.

Yet, what a blessing we enjoyed,
To have him for this while,
His vision that showed us the way,
His broad and joyful smile.

He taught us to be in love with life,
Despite life's all too frequent pain.
He'd change life's bitter chunks of coal,
Into the diamonds of life's gain.

Always faithful in his walk with God,
He held in esteem his fellow man,
He desired for all the higher way,
That God offers freely in his plan.

Yea, and chief among his virtues,
Where he most resembled God above,
Was in the way he held those nearest,
In his honest heartfelt love.

This Leatherneck, this steel-trap mind,
This heart as big as all outdoors,
His feet now march beyond our reach,
But he has left a path for mine and yours.

# On Heaven's Path Sublime

The road through life to heaven's home,
Is for some a long and climbing trail,
While others come by a winding path,
Through woods and troubled vale.

Yet in the end whether steep or curved,
Each must reach the self-same pass,
For 'tis only by the narrow-straight gate,
That one enters into that life that last.

That gate of course in Jesus Christ,
Who meets each traveler along the way,
And invites each one to walk with him,
From here to God's eternal day.

Some he meets in life's darkest woods,
Amid the briars and tempter's snare.
While others he finds in sunny fields,
Of life's joys and pleasures fair.

It matters not which road we're on,
When Jesus intercepts our way,
What matters is that when he does,
We walk with him to God's new day.

Back along Mike's winding trail,
In some vale or a rocky climb,
Jesus came and walked with him,
Now he walks heaven's path sublime.

## Now Does Soar His Soul

He watched the soaring object glide,
Across the morning sky,
The plain he'd built with his own hand,
That at his command did fly.

The controls he held to signals send,
He used with a master's skill,
The plain he had with precision built,
Did respond exactly to his will.

So too the Master Pilot of our soul,
Does watch our spirit climb,
When at last our heart and will,
We to his control resign.

For he has made us for himself,
And commands to soar our soul,
When we in faith receive his grace,
And yield our lives to his control.

So the Master Pilot watched him rise,
As on high his spirit glides,
Upon the wings of eternal life,
That the grace of Christ supplies.

Dr. C.R. Hill, Jr.

# Send Back the Angel's Song

Look there!
See the lighted square.
It's nearly Christmas,
Can't you feel it in the air?

Well then,
Lay hold the Christmas joy.
There is no news so black or bad,
That can the Christmas hope destroy.

Hear that?
'Tis the angel's carol on high,
They herald the Christ, God's infant Son,
Born that men no more shall die

Gone home.
That is all that Jimmy has done.
Gone home to be with God,
And greet God's Savior Son.

Trust God,
For yet your heart will sing.
And with the angels send back the song,
That will make the heavens ring.

## In Tribute to a Peacemaker

Blessed are the peacemakers,
So says the Word of God,
They shall be called the sons,
To whom the Father gives the nod.

So another son has gone,
From our midst to heaven's shore,
Where with the Father in his house,
Peace reigns forevermore.

Yet we recall him fondly here,
For his firm and gentle way,
How with Boudreaux and Thibodaux,
He'd make smooth the roughest day.

A man of statue very large,
Yet of heart much larger still,
And all devoted to one end,
That was to do the Father's will.

Miss him? Yes, of course we do,
Though he has hardly taken leave,
From our presence here below,
So our hearts are bound to greave.

But the tears that we are shedding now,
Will be quickly turned away,
When from the halls of heaven –"Peace,"
We hear that Cajun accent say.

Dr. C.R. Hill, Jr.

# A Promise Whispered Soft

She never saw the light of earth,
Yet darkness she knew not,
For she never left the light of heaven,
Nor the face of God forgot.

We never got to hold her hand,
Or watch her the first step take,
For she never let go of Jesus' hand,
Her full journey here to make.

She was a promise whispered soft,
Of still other lives to come,
If you will carry on in love,
And trust in God's dear Son.

So don't despair if it is love you share,
But with faith in Jesus walk,
As daily in the garden of prayer,
You each with him do talk.

And always know as on you go,
That you have not sustained a loss.
Your heavenly treasure has just increased,
For Jesus has redeemed her by his cross.

## Treasure in Heaven

No greater love than this can be,
Than a person life to another give,
That one give up their flesh and blood,
So a fellow traveler their life may live.

Ah, when one who has been thus blessed,
Reaches at last life's finish line,
They know they've seen in a selfless act,
Reflected clear God's love divine.

'Twas this not the way with Doss and Lynn?
Did not each one's heart for the other beat?
Yea, 'twas by her strength his race was run,
Until by grace he did the course complete.

Now has the gulf between them come,
With her in time and him beyond,
But naught can brake that tie that binds,
The love of God that has made them one.

Yea time shall wane lake a passing dream,
That fades from mind at the brake of day,
But love that binds to kindred souls,
Will forever in heaven a treasure stay.

Dr. C.R. Hill, Jr.

## Gods Eternal Day

He calmly took the news,
That no one wants to hear,
The finish of his life on earth,
Was drawing very near.

We hoped the news was wrong,
Or could some how be reversed,
But in his spirit he really knew,
And braced against the worst.

Yet for the worst it would not be,
Of that he was quite sure.
The worst would be to linger here,
And greater pain and sorrow endure.

What he knew would be the best,
Would be to walk with Jesus home.
And live forever in God's grace,
That here on earth he'd know.

Now free of pain and bathed in love,
The joy of life in full he knows,
His sins forgiven his body healed,
Where the River of Life forever flows.

So now in courage may you walk on.
Let his calm assurance lead your way,
Soon you shall reach life's river's edge,
And cross to God's eternal day.

## Sailing Glad and Graceful

In the hush that marks the fading night,
And heralds the rising sun,
A frail but steady ship set sail,
Her eternal voyage begun.

No band to play as she sets out,
No friends to stand and wave,
Her unassuming sails unfurl,
To her pilot sure and brave.

The shores of time grow distant now,
Though her mark is firmly made,
For she crossed the treacherous sands of life,
In the tracks her Master laid.

With heaven's portals now in view,
She's sailing glad and graceful,
Her captain's voice rings out, "Well done,
My child so meek and faithful."

Dr. C.R. Hill, Jr.

# Until the Children All Get Home

I rode last evening by Granddad's place,
It doesn't look the same today.
That driveway used to go on forever,
Now it is but a little way.

The porch that used to wrap around,
Has been completely changed,
White columns now the entrance guard,
The whole place is rearranged.

But Granny Ward and Granddad,
Haven't lived out there for years,
They long ago have moved beyond,
This lower land of tears.

Ah, but Tony passed by Granddad's,
Several days ago.
The mansion where they're living now,
Is quite some place I know.

All the kin folks there were gathered,
Like when he was just a boy,
Their faces were all smiling,
Their hearts were filled with joy.

They all called out to greet him,
Thad was the first to hug his neck.
It was every thing he had imagined,
Just as Jesus taught him to expect.

From the kitchen came smells of dinner,
The table was neatly set,
But the dinner bell was still silent,
For all the children weren't home yet.

Down that driveway they keep looking,
For the next one to come home,
While their prayers they keep on lifting,
For us who yet down here do roam.

## From the House on Hampton Street

Look now,
At this house on Hampton Street,
She is gone who hosted boarders,
That would frequent here to eat.

Seems strange,
To see it empty and alone,
For few remain who can recall,
When this was not her home.

Ninety-nine,
A long time to live on earth,
But ninety-nine is just the start,
For one with heaven's birth.

Lemma's moved,
After so long on Hampton Street,
She has taken up her heavenly home,
And with Jesus gone to eat.

Dr. C.R. Hill, Jr.

## Today in Heaven Found

"Free at last, free at last,
Free from suffering, pain, and woe.
Free at last, free at last,
From death and to life I go."

O' that's the cry of the joyful soul,
Who in Jesus finds peace with God.
Though to hear on rejoice at death,
Does to this world seem quit odd.

But to the soul who has Jesus known,
It is the long awaited dream,
To shed earth's bondage here below,
And with the light of heaven beam.

So it is that our brother here,
Has the chains of flesh laid down,
His suffering over, his pain all gone,
He is today in heaven found.

In robes of white at Jesus' feet,
His losses on earth more than restored,
He shall with saints forever rejoice,
In Jesus Christ his risen Lord.

And there he waits for you and me,
With the host by Jesus there redeemed,
To welcome us each one by one,
Who of God's kingdom here have dreamed.

## Until You Reach Heaven's Home and Me

The road of life is of a different length,
For every traveler here,
For some heaven's gates are a distant view,
For some they loom quite near.

They said my road would be so short,
That I'd never come to know,
The joys of life and love on earth,
Before it would be my time to go.

And true enough it is over too soon,
Yet not before I had my taste,
Of the wonders of a loving home,
And my Lord's redeeming grace.

I'm sorry mom and dad for this,
That I have to heaven you out run,
But dry your tears, I'll meet you here,
When your road on earth is done.

I'm glad I had the time I did,
To spend on earth with you,
I learned how love can overcome,
When others think you're through.

'Tis the faith that I received from you,
That let me surpass each earthly goal,
That now I render back to you,
So it may you in your grief console.

You taught me how by faith in Christ,
I could in life a conquer be,
So now hold fast the faith you taught,
Until you reach heaven's home and me.

Dr. C.R. Hill, Jr.

## Come Home with Me Today

Good morning, Lord.
I've strayed too far from home;
Now the road that leads back there,
Seems too hard to walk alone.

Look here, Lord.
I've written in the sand,
Each and every sinful thing,
I've committed by my hand.

Forgive me, Lord,
For these sins I write today.
It seems amid the maze of life,
I turned and lost my way.

Be near them, Lord.
Stand by in loved ones' sorrow,
And by your healing hope and love,
May they receive new life tomorrow.

"Come here my son,
And take my nail pierced hand,
For I have cleansed and washed away,
Your sins upon the sand.

You turned it's true.
I know you lost your way.
But I died that you could live,
So come home with me today.

## The Voyager's Rest

Some ships sail on peaceful seas,
And dock on pleasant shores,
For others the sea is often rough,
As the tempest steady roars.

Yet when he who the storm has known,
His voyage's end does reach,
He then does all the more rejoice,
On heaven's golden beach.

So our brother's voyage has ended,
Far too soon for us of course,
But the gale that drove his ship,
Was an unrelenting force.

Now that he the waves has ridden,
To heaven's tranquil port,
He is rejoicing with loved ones there,
In his Savior's welcome court.

There'll be no more storm tossed seas,
No tempest winds or angry waves,
For he was safely born across,
By Jesus Christ who saves.

So you his fellow voyagers now,
Have still your journeys to complete.
Chart the way Jesus made for you,
To his Father's mercy seat.

Dr. C.R. Hill, Jr.

## The Captain of Souls

I've sailed my ship through a turbulent sea,
Through the waves from winds and wake.
'Tis storms that breed the waves of winds,
The others were waves that I did make.

'Tis not a thing for which to be ashamed,
To make some waves through life,
But oft' upon life's trackless sea,
Waves can obscure one's way with strife.

Like a seaman lost in those swells and swirl,
I was feeling confused and alone,
When through the mists and raging brine,
The Captain of Souls came and led me home.

Look!, now I walk by that crystal sea,
Spreading tranquil before God's throne,
And the Captain of Souls is walking with me,
Imparting more peace than I've ever known.

I know that the sea is still raging for you,
As you yet deal with the hurtful waves,
But the Captain of Souls is sailing with you,
And from the storms of life's seas he saves.

So set your course by his rising star,
By his compass of love fix your heart.
You'll safely sail to life's distant shore,
And there we never again shall part.

## The Little While

There comes to us the little while;
The time when we must part,
And for a season now my love,
I know it breaks your heart.

I don't know why two lives in time,
Must reach the parting ways,
When one goes home to be with God,
While the other partner stays.

Perhaps he's got our mansion through,
But needs my woman's touch.
Or perhaps he's got some work for you,
That I couldn't help with much.

No matter, love, it's just a while,
Your grieving season's brief.
And, Dear, you know the love we share,
Is worth a little grief.

I know that you will not despair,
God won't let you walk alone.
I'll wait for you just over here,
Inside our heavenly home.

# In Unbroken Step

A man of God went home today,
His last appointment done.
He left behind this veil of flesh,
His race of life well run.

A man of God went home today,
From a life spent under call,
To preach, to move, to give himself,
In love to great and small.

A man of God went home today,
A saint advanced in years.
Though loved ones grieve to let him go,
Their hope overcomes their tears.

A man of God went home today;
To receive the crown he'd won,
And the mantle of his service here,
Passed to his Preacher Son.

## Yonder Heaven's Gate

Daddy took his flight today,
On the wings of the morning's storms,
His long trail finely ended here,
And he took flight to Jesus' arms.

Long was the trail he walked with us,
Far beyond four score and ten.
O' he life's secrets had unlocked,
For he knew that Jesus walked with him.

Two sons before him had walked on,
His loving wife had too,
You sons who follow mark well his path,
For they wait up the trail for you.

Indeed the day draws near to all,
When the trails of earth shall end,
And all who in this life look to Christ,
Will together walk again.

Take now the time to shed a tear,
For sweet memories from here below.
Let those memories inspire your walk,
As onward on your trail you go.

Then let the joy that is up ahead,
Where the others for you wait,
Turn tearful eyes to eyes that laugh,
As you glimpse yonder heaven's gate.

Dr. C.R. Hill, Jr.

## The Echo on the Breeze

The keys are resting silent now,
Her music here has ceased,
She moved to be at home with God,
When she her hold on earth released.

Her friends assembled to bid farewell,
Remembering that bygone day,
When her music filled the morning air,
As they approached God's house to pray.

They remember too the quiet way,
That she with steady caring love,
Pointed toward the Son of God,
And his path to life above.

O I still see her sitting there,
In her house beside the road,
Waiting for a friend to stop,
And lighten their day's load.

That house is standing vacant now,
With no friend who waits within,
But in a mansion by streets of gold,
They will visit with her again.

And though her music here has ceased,
Still on the Sunday morning breeze,
Friends who loved her the echo hear,
Of her hands upon the keys.

## Crossing Time

I talked with her not long ago,
For the first time in a while.
I'd visited her at other times,
When she could only smile.

But when I last saw her awake,
Her voice was clear and strong.
We talked that day of crossing time,
She knew it would not be long.

Several things she wanted said,
When we came to celebrate her life,
And the song they sang on that day,
Jim took her to be his wife.

She wanted everyone to know,
That wherever in life they be,
None could them from God remove,
Nor is there a need he does not see.

So learn she said to depend on him,
And not on yourself rely,
For no matter where you are in life,
God's grace will you supply.

Then on his all sufficient love,
May you learn you can depend,
So when your crossing time arrives,
You'll know it is a beginning not an end.

Dr. C.R. Hill, Jr.

# The Wrencher

I'd seen that old blue truck of his,
Parked there beneath the shed.
Sometimes I'd see it out and about,
Some small cargo in the bed.

Mostly though as I recall,
I'd just see it sitting there,
A reminder of the way he was,
Always ready for some load to bear.

They really were not big things;
At least as measured by most folks,
But like a wheel that's held in true,
By so many tiny spokes.

It was in many tiny ways each day,
He would quietly lend support,
That now has elevated him so high,
In heaven's honor court.

Is that not the thing that Jesus taught,
With his servant style of life,
That it is the humble faithful servant,
Who wrenches victory out of strife?

# O Heed the Somber Notes

The somber notes of taps,
Drifting across the hallowed ground,
In tribute to the faithful souls,
Who would for country life lay down.

In freedom yet awake we live,
For the sacrifice they would make,
And still so often we disregard,
Or their risk too lightly take.

O' may we all on this hallowed day,
Hear those notes so crisp and clear,
And devote ourselves to carry on,
The ideals these held so dear.

Dr. C.R. Hill, Jr.

## One Desire Alone She Held

When mother left this earthly room,
And closed the door on life below,
She firmly grasped the hand of God,
And to her heavenly home did go.

Oh how for this she had deeply longed,
To be with her loved ones there.
To leave the narrow confines of earth,
For heaven's wonders beyond compare.

The joy she brought we'll truly miss,
Her sharp whit and pleasant smile.
Her love she always made so clear,
Yes we will miss these for a while.

Yet I believe the time is short,
Even should we live beyond her years,
When we will be with her again,
Where only joy shall bid our tears.

And until that time for us shall come,
It is for us to find and trace her trail,
For it was Jesus' path of faith and love,
That has taken her to life beyond the veil.

Ah, one desire alone she held,
Above her wish in heaven to be,
That in due time we each will come,
So she in heaven shall our faces see.

## Walking with Jesus at Dawn

I've taken the wings of the morning,
And flown at long last to my home.
I've walked the long highway of aging,
Now to the ageless dimensions I've gone.

When I'm laid to rest at life's evening,
My soul will be singing life's song,
For God held my hand through the shadows,
Of the midnights that lingered so long.

So grieve not my passing my darlings,
For to weep o'er my passing is wrong.
My home is now waiting in heaven,
Where my Walter has already gone.

I'll arise in the morning of heaven,
And bow down before God on his throne.
Then I'll take up my new life forever;
Singing praises with that heavenly throng.

For in the sunrise and mist of the daybreak,
To the endless blue skies far beyond,
I left earth for heaven this morning,
And went walking with Jesus at dawn.

Dr. C.R. Hill, Jr.

## The Father's Homeward Call

How many times before,
Had he heard his father say,
"Time to come home now son."
And he'd be on his way.

So it was that afternoon,
As he was heading home,
His heavenly Father called his name,
In that voice since a child he'd known.

"It is time to come home now son."
So to us he said, "Goodbye,"
And went home to be with Jesus,
In his home beyond the sky.

For those of us he leaves behind,
It feels like he has gone too soon.
It wasn't in life's evening he left,
He had hardly reached life's noon.

Yet heaven doesn't measure time,
As we measure down here below,
It is when God has the table set for us,
That comes for us our time to go.

God knows the empty place you feel,
How you hurt deep in your heart.
And each of you in God's time will hear,
"Come, and never more from loved ones part."

This is the promise that Jesus gives us,
That while life here is all to brief,
Life eternal is the gift he brings,
To all who in him have placed belief.

# Jean

"John", they say of Bible fame,
Is by the eagle's face portrayed,
She can fly directly into the sun,
And not be dazzled or dismayed.

"Jean", appropriately enough his name,
On who's faith we did so rely,
Has taken flight to be with God,
And to walk with Christ on high.

Long he walked with us below,
A friend and light along our way.
He taught us we should expect results,
When we bowed head and heart to pray.

He really claimed no special power,
This man of faith and courage rare,
He merely knew God to faithful be,
When he promised to hear and answer prayer.

Now he sleeps, this man of God,
On who's firm faith we did rely.
He who's prayers ascended on our behalf,
Now intercedes for us on high.

Dr. C.R. Hill, Jr.
# To The Master of the March

Thin puffs of clouds like dark shadows with silver halos,
Slowly sweep across the platinum face of November's moon in full.
Easing her way westward along her prehistoric path,
This radiant light has already settled behind the distant treetops,
Treetops whose nearly leafless limbs stand silhouetted,
Dark and melancholy like in the moon's soft light.

Closer by the straight forked trunk of a white oak tree,
Stands framed in the gable window like a giant tuning fork.
Its "V" too narrow to resemble a good sling shot staff,
Like those we boys used to cut for ourselves and string with strips of inner
tube.
Still with a little imagination it could be thought of as such.
And the moon like a large shining marble that some boy has just flung out
into space.

The long restless night is waning.
Soon—in less than an hour now—the trees on the other side of the house,
Will be silhouetted in the gray light of coming day.
Too early to read the sky for sure, but my guess is it will be a red sunrise,
Such as sailors tell us speak of coming rain.

Rain is needed—even now to be desired—despite the gorgeous days,
Of clear blue skies and temperatures that feel just right,
Just right for a little sleeve on the arm,
but no contending with cumbersome coats,
And hats that blow off in the whipping wind.

Morning is coming.  Soon now, and with it maybe rain.
Days come that way.  Some born from the womb of moon light,
To bring bright skies with sunlight.
Some likewise born to bring refreshing rain.
And we—we are blessed to see each one come.
Some days bring the reign of sadness and heaviness of heart.
Some bring joy and gladness, and the peace of things gone right.
And we—we are blessed to see each one come.

# To Walk in Heaven's Light

For each day comes as a solitary marcher along the prehistoric path.
Each one passing slowly steadily westward,
As we enjoy the company they bring then bid them at evening time our adieu.
And we—we are blessed to see each one come,
And blessed to see each one pass again tonight.

We are blessed the more because we know that behind this march of days,
There stands the one who beats the drum counting out the cadence
by which they keep in step.
The Master of the March who has each moment marked.
'Tis he, the Master of the March, who knows the day and hour,
When he will call to each of us, "Fall in!"
Then we will march with him along the prehistoric path,
On our steady westward journey where day will know no end.

# Poem Index

| Poem | Name | Page |
|---|---|---|
| A Champion Now At Home | Hammond, Graydon | 104 |
| A Chat On Heaven's Porch | Ray, Marjorie Pague | 192 |
| A Dream for Children's Sake | Martin, J. Lamar | 150 |
| A Familiar Home and Crown | Langston, James Donald | 141 |
| A Father's Steps | Nale, Frank Winton | 175 |
| A Fisherman's Farewell | Fincher, Jack Chamber Jr | 84 |
| A Giant I Recall | Brown, James Maxwell Jr | 32 |
| A House Not Made With Hands | Fuetus, Betty | 89 |
| A Kinsman of the King | Smith Ray | 214 |
| A Lady Following Jesus | Claxton, Frances Rowan | 57 |
| A Light Still Shining | Goodman, Bessie Mays | 95 |
| A Man from Heaven Sent | DeVan, Jim | 74 |
| A Man Like His Mountains of Home | Lewis, Hugh Neal | 144 |
| A Mountain Flower Blooming | Fincher, Frances | 83 |
| A Name That Stood For More | Polk, C. O. Jack | 186 |
| A Promise Whispered Soft | Velandia, Anais Marie | 232 |
| A Queen In Servant's Attire | Anderson, Martha Marie | 4 |
| A Ransomed Spirit's Prayer | Shankles, Velma | 211 |
| A Runner's Early Finish | Hannah, Seth | 107 |
| A Saint Has Transferred Home | Brandenburg, Mabel M | 25 |
| A Saint with No Fear | Hinman, Christine | 124 |
| A Steep from Time to Heave Go | Rooks, Mary Grace | 202 |

Dr. C.R. Hill, Jr.

| Poem | Name | Page |
|---|---|---|
| Across the Finish Line | Burch, Marge | 35 |
| Always Looking Up | Moses, Quentin | 172 |
| Among the Hills of Time | Hill, Carl Richard Sr. | 119 |
| An Airman's Final Flight | Kelly, Howard Rae | 136 |
| An Amplifying Echo | DeVan Jim | 73 |
| An Ode to Valor | Ballenger, Bill | 14 |
| Anchors for the Soul | Richards, Tracey Gail | 199 |
| Around the Last Corner | Powell, Gladys | 187 |
| Around the Upward Bend | Beck, Paul | 19 |
| As the Eagle's Strength Renew | Cantrell, Roger Lynn | 43 |
| As the Saints in Order Go | Lovell, Nell Cook | 148 |
| At Heaven's Morning Roll Call | Duncan, Major W. L. | 75 |
| At Heaven's Open Door | Smith, Kathryn | 218 |
| At Home Where the Angle Sings | Cantrell, Etta White | 42 |
| At the Master Servant's Feet | Austin, Allene | 9 |
| At the Water's Edge | Hill, Louise V. | 122 |
| Before The Crystal Sea | Stackhouse, Jennie T. | 221 |
| Beholding God's Eternal Dawn | Cannon, David Lee | 39 |
| Beyond Autumn's Clear Blue Sky | Roberts, Virginia Lee | 200 |
| Beyond the Far Horizon | Shackelford, Stinson | 208 |
| Beyond the Fields of Brown | Bankston Benny & Frances | 15 |
| Beyond the Forest Dark | Carlton, Christopher Edward | 44 |
| Beyond The Whispered Years | Arnold, Sara Barber | 6 |
| Birch Cook's Store | Cook, Hugh Burch | 61 |

| Poem | Name | Page |
|---|---|---|
| Born to Rise Eternal | Nichols, William | 176 |
| By Nature's Ancient Bridge | Cathy, Louise R. | 50 |
| By the Christmas Baby's Voice | Parham, Ellen Irene | 178 |
| Christmas Day in the Evening | Harris, William Glaze | 111 |
| Come Home 'Preacher' | McGarity, Harold L. | 156 |
| Come Home Now Child | Jones, Vera May Haley | 133 |
| Come Home with Me Today | Wesley, Rick | 240 |
| Crossing the Silver Tide | Sellars, Mike | 206 |
| Crossing Time | Yarbrough, Kathy | 247 |
| Diamonds on the Cheek | Gray, Charlotte | 97 |
| Each One He Made His Own | Bacon John | 11 |
| Evening Time at Home | Crow, Donald | 65 |
| Evening's Homeward Call | Chandler, Lou Anne | 53 |
| Fast in the Master's Hand | Clifford, Melinda Lewis | 58 |
| Finally Home | Myatt, Edna R. | 173 |
| Fishing With Big Bob | Lanford, Robert A. | 140 |
| Fishing With God's Son | Halpin, Frank Sr | 100 |
| Flying | Barger, William and Mitch | 18 |
| Forever at Christmas Home | Stitt, Jimmy | 222 |
| Friends with a Saint | Peek, Roy | 182 |
| From All His Labors Rested | Gunter, Jim | 99 |
| From Better Jesus Knowing. | Shankles, Jean | 209 |
| From Papa's Cotton Basket | Caldwell, Ellene Louise | 38 |
| From the House on Hampton Street | Ward, Lemma | 237 |

| Poem | Name | Page |
|---|---|---|
| From the Top of the Hill | Brisendine, John William | 29 |
| From the Topside Down | Caldwell, Andrew Leonard | 37 |
| From the Trackless Wood Emerged | McDaniel, Bobby | 154 |
| From Water's Edge to Heaven's Shore | Moore, Betty | 167 |
| God's Eternal Living Game | Smith, David | 216 |
| God's Home of Endless Day | Haygood, Ellis | 117 |
| God's Stage Where Life Goes On | Attaway, Johnny | 8 |
| God's Tomorrow | Krueger, August | 139 |
| Gods Eternal Day | Walter, David | 234 |
| Going By His Place | Miller, Carl | 165 |
| Going on in the Greatness of Grace | Shankles, Loyd Bascom | 210 |
| Gone To Be With God | Carroll, Odell Edwin | 45 |
| Grieve Not My Love | Pickett, Donald Lamar | 185 |
| He Lives | Strickland, William Andrew (Drew) | 226 |
| He Played the Game for God | Hogan, Jack | 125 |
| He Will Forever Each One Know | Anderson, Wendell | 5 |
| Heaven Bound On the Evening Breeze | Edge, Anne | 76 |
| Heaven's Diamonds | Amos, Lydia Jo | 2 |
| Heaven's Gain | DeMore, Eleanor | 71 |
| Heaven's Glad Tomorrow | Gibson, Horace Eugene Jr. | 91 |
| Heaven's Porch Light | Elliott, Frankie | 78 |
| Heaven's Summer Garden Room | Peterson, Sylvia | 183 |
| Her Gold Refined | Reed, Sherry | 193 |

| Poem | Name | Page |
|---|---|---|
| Her Mansion on Heaven's Side | Joiner, Julia May | 131 |
| Her Songs Will Keep On Ringing | Bryant, Pam | 33 |
| His Love Runs With You Still | Hightower, Clinton Sr. | 118 |
| His Spirit Sought the Sky | Smith, Richard Jackson | 215 |
| His View from Above the Clouds | Reisert, Rick Alan | 195 |
| Home by the Higher Way | Rhodes, Becky | 197 |
| I'll Meet You At The River | Gardner, Jane Elliott | 90 |
| I'll See You Again | Milford, Norma Ann | 162 |
| If for a Moment One Believes | Davis, Jami E | 69 |
| In Celebration of Life | Smith, Mary Jean | 213 |
| In Gardens of Glory | Hammarstrom, Flow M. | 103 |
| In God's Distant Promise Land | McCurry Shirley Ann | 153 |
| In God's Eternal Book | Briscoe, Ruth Evans | 28 |
| In God's Homecoming Court. | Langston, Mary Jane | 142 |
| In God's Never Ending Day | Harbin, Winfred | 108 |
| In Heaven with Her Pilot | Sawyer, Eugenia Hodges | 204 |
| In Heaven's Arms | Sparks, John Sr. | 219 |
| In Heaven's Finished Room | Foster, Emerson Parks | 88 |
| In Heaven's Mansion Grand | Cates, Laura Hamilton | 48 |
| In Heaven's Pastures Green | Scott, Brenelle Mobley | 205 |
| In My Eternal Strength | Ferrell, Charles Maurice | 81 |
| In Strength She Now Is Dancing | Dettner, Marry Alice | 72 |
| In the Echo of Heart's Love | Jones, Jane Colleen Schalf | 134 |
| In the Father's Loving Palm | Miller, Anita Rooks | 164 |

Dr. C.R. Hill, Jr.

| Poem | Name | Page |
|---|---|---|
| In the House His Love Designed | Clark, Virginia Ray V. A. | 56 |
| In the House of God's Abode | Fife, Sue Weaver | 82 |
| In the Hymns of Hope and Heaven | Rowland, Barbara | 203 |
| In the Life Beyond Tomorrow | Morris, Danny | 171 |
| In the Light that Christmas Brings | Cox, Jerry | 64 |
| In the Memory of Her Love | Clark, Diana Kay | 54 |
| In the Resurrection Morning | Naffziger, Beth | 174 |
| In Tribute to a Peacemaker | Underwood, Daniel Patrick | 231 |
| In Tribute to a Steel Magnolia | Haney, Meena | 106 |
| In Unbroken Step | Woods, Harry | 244 |
| In You Her Song Lives On | Dalais, Rosa Emma | 67 |
| It Is Finished | Britt, Terri | 30 |
| Jean | Zachary, Jean M. | 253 |
| Joyce's Song | McDaniel, Joyce Elizabeth | 155 |
| Lady Jane | Carter, Jane | 47 |
| Life at Road's End | Berwald Annabelle | 20 |
| Like the Master Archer's Arrow | Carter, Edward P | 46 |
| Living on Life's Second Page | Kimball, Vivian Elizabeth | 137 |
| Marching Orders Received | McVay, Birch G | 157 |
| Margaret's Song | Gorham, Margret Louise | 96 |
| Measure Twice, Saw Once | Phillips, Aaron Paul | 184 |
| Moved Home | Strawn, Grace | 224 |
| Now Does Soar His Soul | Terrill, Ray | 229 |
| O Heed the Somber Notes | Yeckering, Josh | 249 |

| Poem | Name | Page |
|---|---|---|
| Off Again | Corbett, Anne Elizabeth | 62 |
| On A Bright November Day | Lathem, Dot | 143 |
| On Heaven's Golden Street | Morgan, James H. "Jay" | 170 |
| On Heaven's Path Sublime | Tarrh, Francis Michael | 228 |
| On Morning's Wings | Glass, Allen Howard | 93 |
| On Silent Wings He Flew | Reynolds, Roy Henry | 196 |
| On the Crossing of Jordin | Metcalf, Jordin Merit | 161 |
| On the Death of a Teacher | Brodnax, Sarah Leora | 31 |
| On the Passing of a Friend | Hutchings, Gretta | 127 |
| On the Wings of Evening's Wind | Hardeman, Elizabeth | 109 |
| On the Wings of Fluid Grace | Crumpler, George A. | 66 |
| On the Wings of God | Ray, Dorothy | 190 |
| On The Wings of Grace | Ford, James Richard | 87 |
| One By One on Heaven's Shore | Rooks, James | 201 |
| One Desire Alone She Held | Yohe, Iris Hope | 250 |
| Papa's House | Gleaton, William Horace | 94 |
| Passing Through | Moore, Marion Helm | 168 |
| Precious in God's Sight | Milton, Sallie | 166 |
| Rejoicing on the Dance Floor | Hattendorf, Wilbur S | 114 |
| Sailing From the Shores of Time | Harris, Virginia McAdams | 110 |
| Sailing Glad and Graceful | *Wander, Marelon* | 235 |
| Sailing with the Evening Tide | Hime, Virginia Nelson | 123 |
| Salute to a Christian Gentleman | McCurry Harris | 152 |
| Salute to a Quiet Man | Coan, Charles W. | 60 |

| Poem | Name | Page |
|---|---|---|
| Semper Fi, Always Faithful | Stubbs, Robert S. II | 227 |
| Send Back the Angel's Song | Turner, James Roy (Jimmy) | 230 |
| She Danced into Heaven with a Smile | Chambers, Anna Elizabeth | 51 |
| She Walks in Heaven's Light | Hill, Jacqueline (Jackie) W. | 121 |
| Sitting Delighted at God's Table | Ray, Joseph Pierce, Jr. | 191 |
| Someday Will Be Homecoming | Hamilton, George | 102 |
| Taken Flight with the Autumn Leaves | Rainer, Robert Andrew | 189 |
| Taking Leave in Autumn | Ellis, Marie | 79 |
| The Anchors of God's Grace | Biddle Carol | 21 |
| The Anchors of God's Grace | Harrison, Robert Michael | 112 |
| The Angel to Us Loaned | Bowden, Aubrey Marie | 24 |
| The Artist's Hands | Stone, Helen | 223 |
| The Biggest Race of All | London, Melvin Dale | 146 |
| The Call of the Distant Lights | Arnold, William C. | 7 |
| The Candy Man's Gone Home | Strawn, William Laurie | 225 |
| The Captain of Souls | Willis, Charles G. | 242 |
| The Captain's Voyage | Stackhouse, H. Collin | 220 |
| The Christ-Learned Way | Richards, Ellis Hampton | 198 |
| The Crossing | Bridges, Martha Franklin | 27 |
| The Crown Through Jesus Won | Reider, Josh | 194 |
| The Doorway to God's Best | Smith, Glenda Echols | 217 |
| The Echo of His Soul | Martin, James L. (Jim) | 149 |
| The Echo on the Breeze | Yarbrough Doris | 246 |

| Poem | Name | Page |
|------|------|------|
| The Father's Homeward Call | Young, Michael Neil | 252 |
| The Fording of Heaven's Stream | Haney, J. B. Jr. | 105 |
| The Garden Gate | Bagwell, Wayne Sr | 13 |
| The Gates of Heaven Gained | DeMore, Coyle A | 70 |
| The Graduate | Clark, J. Norman | 55 |
| The Harbor of God's Arms | Breeding, Earnie | 26 |
| The Heavenly Voyager | Shaw, Edgar | 212 |
| The Home Jesus Built Above | Peacock, Dorothy | 179 |
| The Home with Heaven's View | Hull, Byrd | 126 |
| The Homecoming | Jones, George | 132 |
| The Homecoming | Mercer, Elizabeth "Judy" | 160 |
| The Homeland of the Soul | Blumenaus, John | 22 |
| The Homeward Leading Lane | Jago, Norman | 128 |
| The Impressions of a Saint | Linch, Kathryn | 145 |
| The Keel That Keeps Us True | Cates, Paul Sr. | 49 |
| The Lady Has Gone Home | Jago, Vivian | 129 |
| The Little While | Wilson, Gladys | 243 |
| The Master of Mended Souls | Moore, Paul Wesley | 169 |
| The Model Man | Price, J. P. | 188 |
| The Music of His Life | Boling, Fred | 23 |
| The Music of His Life | Farrell, Harry G. | 80 |
| The Passing of a Lady | Peek, Dot | 181 |
| The Priceless Jewel | Bannister, Jewell Wyatt | 17 |
| The Quiet Man and Heaven's Son | Buffington, Herbert Luther Jr. | 34 |

| Poem | Name | Page |
|---|---|---|
| The Resetting of the Sails | Hill, Daniel Henry | 120 |
| The Resting of a Soldier | Anderson, James R | 3 |
| The Reunion | Shackelford, Mildred Smith | 207 |
| The Ripples In God's Palm | Alexander, John Lafayette | 1 |
| The Runner | Bankston, Joel B | 16 |
| The Sailing of a Saint | Hawkins, James Robert Sr. | 115 |
| The Sendoff of A Friend | McClure Earl | 151 |
| The Shadow of a Giant | Milford, Turk John | 163 |
| The Summit Reached | Chambers, Mary Knight | 52 |
| The Teacher and the Saint | Butler, Mimi Jo | 36 |
| The Voice of the Morning Breeze | Owen, John Walker | 177 |
| The Voyager's Rest | White, Milton Thomas | 241 |
| The Well Blessed Man | Joyner, Charles Johnny | 135 |
| The Wrencher | Yawn, Aubrey Dewitt | 248 |
| This Hero | King, Arnold Nathan | 138 |
| Through Ageless Seasons Singing | Fincher, Katherine | 85 |
| To a 'Homegoing' Queen | Cannon, Sharon | 41 |
| To God's Eternal Day | Gray, Veachel Loyd | 98 |
| To Heaven's Shore | Hamilton, Fannie | 101 |
| To the Master of the March | To Those Whose Poems Were Not Available for this Collection | 254 |
| Today in Heaven Found | Warren, Steve | 238 |
| Today in Heaven I Wear a Smile | Hayes, Courtney | 116 |
| Tomorrow's Heavenly Morning Dew | Jinks, Sarah E. | 130 |

| Poem | Name | Page |
|---|---|---|
| Treasure in Heaven | Wallace, Hubert (Doss) | 233 |
| Until Reunion Day | McVay, Mary Elizabeth | 159 |
| Until the Children All Get Home | Ward, Thaddeus Anthony | 236 |
| Until You Reach Heaven's Home | Welch, Hunter | 239 |
| Walking with Jesus at Dawn | Young, Charlotte | 251 |
| Well Done | Bagwell Randall | 12 |
| When Came Her Crossing Time | Cowan, Geneva Emma | 63 |
| When the Heart Will Sing and Dance | Clifford, Sandra Gail | 59 |
| When you Meet in Heaven's Dawn | Edge, Carl | 77 |
| Where Life is Young Again | Austin, John Byron | 10 |
| Where Saints Immortal Stand | Lovell, Forrest W. | 147 |
| Whispers of Reveille | McVay, Hilda L. | 158 |
| With Eagle's Wings She Flies | Hasty, Hazel Bonnie | 113 |
| With Happy Memories Dear | Gibson, Mary Agnes | 92 |
| With Heaven's Path Conformed | Cannon, Emma Sue Tippens | 40 |
| With Jesus I've Gone Fishing | Daniel, Samuel Jack | 68 |
| With the Christmas Christ Now Gone | Floyd, Mabel Trellis | 86 |
| With the Master Pilot | Peacock, Harry | 180 |
| Yonder Heaven's Gate | Wynn, Lee F. Sr. | 245 |
| A Champion Now At Home | Hammond, Graydon | 104 |

Dr. C. R. Hill, Jr. is an ordained United Methodist Minister in the North Georgia Conference of the United Methodist Church. In addition to his pastoral ministry, He has served on numerous conference and district boards and agencies.

He has written sermons, poems, and articles as well as published four previous books, *Between Two Worlds, Light From Beyond the Veil, Through The Frosted Window,* and *I Talked With Him This Morning.*

C. R. retired from active pastoral ministry at the 2011session of the North Georgian Conference. Since retiring he has been serving as a Hospital Chaplain, Interim Chaplain at Reinhardt University, and as of Annual Conference of 2017 he is currently serving as Pastor of Wesley Chapel United Methodist Church in Dahlonega, Georgia in addition to continuing as a Part-Time Hospital Chaplain at Northside Hospital Cherokee.

C. R. was married to his late wife Jackie for over fifty-four years. They have two children a son and a daughter, a son-in law, and a daughter-in-law, three grandsons, one granddaughter-in-law, and one great-granddaughter.